New-Fangled, Old-Fashioned Bread Puddings

ST. MARTIN'S PRESS

NEW YORK

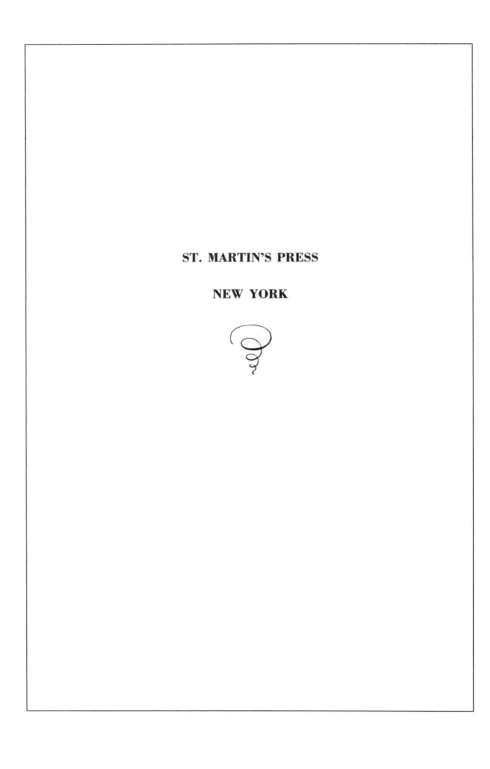

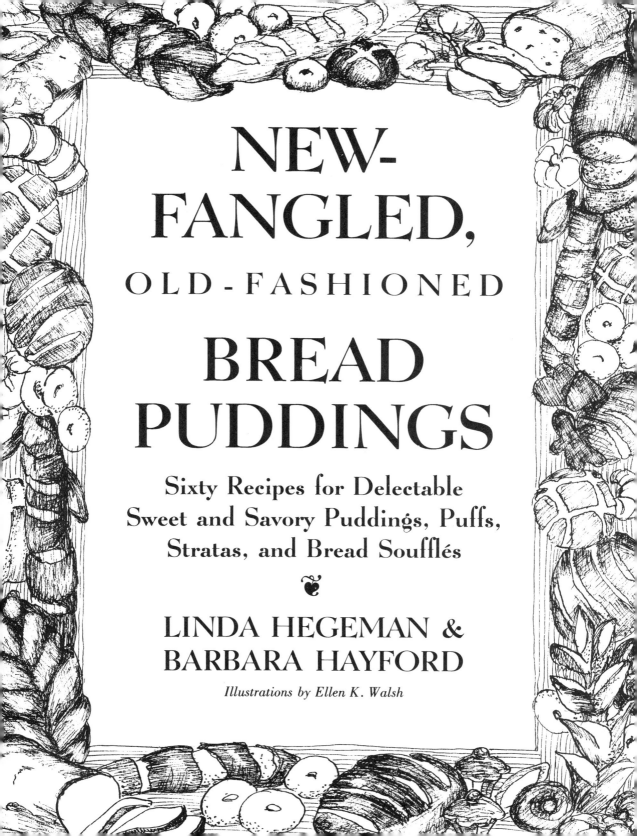

NEW-FANGLED,

OLD-FASHIONED

BREAD PUDDINGS

Sixty Recipes for Delectable Sweet and Savory Puddings, Puffs, Stratas, and Bread Soufflés

❧

LINDA HEGEMAN & BARBARA HAYFORD

Illustrations by Ellen K. Walsh

Library of Congress Cataloging-in-Publication Data

Hegeman, Linda.
New-fangled, old-fashioned bread puddings / Linda Hegeman and
Barbara Hayford.
p.   cm.
ISBN 0-312-10509-6 (pbk.) : $10.95
1. Bread puddings.   I. Hayford, Barbara.   II. Title.
TX773.H37   1994
641.8'64—dc20   *93-36700*
CIP

First Edition: January 1994
10   9   8   7   6   5   4   3   2   1

If you have a favorite bread pudding of your own, or if you have tasted a special bread pudding in a restaurant, we'd love to hear about it. Please write to us at 6109 Spring Mill Road, Indianapolis, Indiana 46208.

Chefs and restaurants whose recipes appear in this book

Johanne Killeen and George Germon, Al Forno (Providence)
Anne Rosenzweig, Arcadia (New York City)
Dawn Bailey, John Ash & Co. (Santa Rosa, California)
Karl "Woody" Will, Auberge du Soleil (Rutherford, California)
Angelica Santos, Barocco Alimentari (New York City)
Kilian B. Weigand, Biba (Boston)
Kitty Sullivan, Cilantros (Del Mar, California)
Steven Keneipp, The Classic Kitchen (Noblesville, Indiana)
Bradley Ogden, Lark Creek Inn (Larkspur, California)
Michael Foley, Printer's Row and Le Perroquet (both Chicago)
Dickie Brennan, Palace Cafe (New Orleans)
Tom Poulsen, Shapiro's Delicatessen and Cafeteria (Indianapolis)
Susan Goss, Something Different (Indianapolis)
Wolfgang Puck, Spago (West Hollywood, California)
Emily Luchetti, Stars (San Francisco)
John Terczak, Tamales Restaurants (Chicago and Highland Park, Illinois)
Peggy A. Elliott, Tulio (Seattle)

Food experts whose comments appear in this book

Marcia Adams, author and TV chef, *Cooking from Quilt Country, Heartland* and *Christmas in the Heartland*
John Ash, Chef/Proprietor, John Ash & Co. (Santa Rosa, California)
Nancy Baggett, author of *The International Chocolate Cookbook*
Lee Bailey, author of *Lee Bailey's Tomatoes*
Bernard Clayton, Jr., author of *Bernard Clayton's Cooking Across America*
Perla Meyers, author of *Perla Meyers' Art of Seasonal Cooking*
Julee Rosso, co-author of *The Silver Palate Cookbooks* and *The New Basics Cookbook*, and author of *Great Good Food—Lucious Lower-Fat Cooking*
Marlene Sorosky, author of *Dessert Lover's Cookbook*

To Ted and Jack, our dear husbands

We thank our families for their patience and good humor.

We thank Marlene Sorosky for her professional guidance in the rigors of cookbook writing.

We thank our agent, Linda Hayes, for seeing the potential in bread puddings and us. Her knowledge and persistence guided us, long distance, for months and months and months.

We thank our editor, Barbara Anderson, for her calm wisdom and unique ability to direct us. She was always accessible.

We thank our contributing chefs for graciously sharing their delicious recipes.

We thank our food celebrities for pausing from their busy schedules to express their personal opinions about bread pudding.

We thank our tasters and testers for their invaluable help in the development of the recipes in this book: Vally Allen, Karen Bailey, Charlene Barnette, Ruth Beyer, Paul Bogigian, Anne Carpenter, Wilmetta Childers, Shirley Christian, Harriet Crockett, Alice Doughty, Tanja Flynn, Ann Frick, Phyllis Gamage, Mary Ann Grogan, Mary Jane Hamburger, Julie Held, Marge Hittle, Kay Ivcevich, Judith James, Margo Jaqua, Betty Keating, Steven Keneipp, Susan Knieser, Jane Kohn, Pat LaCrosse, Eleanor Lopez, Barb McLin, Lin Maggard, Jan Marosky, Jo Meyer, Sandy O'Connor, Pat Orner, Jane Perry, Midge Peschau, Joyce Pruitt, Jean Quinn, Diane Robinson, Lorraine Schlechte, Mary Schuster, Mildred Shands, Joy Sherrill, Rose Simmons, Audrey Stehle, Judy Stusrud, Siter Trudgen, Connie Vinciguerra, Ellen Walsh, Mary Patricia Warneke, Bill Wilson, Jane Anne Wood, Jim Wood, and Zilpha Wood.

CONTENTS

Bread puddings, any kind, are among my most beloved recipes, and I'm thrilled to see this dazzling new collection of old favorites. This book presents a classic dish with scrumptious interpretations."

—*Marcia Adams*
Author and TV Chef, Cooking From Quilt Country, Heartland, *and* Christmas in the Heartland

INTRODUCTION

We love bread puddings!

Bread puddings were not a part of my childhood memories. But from the first bite, bread pudding replaced chocolate cake as my dessert of choice. In my heart, I knew someone was going to write a cookbook entirely about bread pudding and I wanted that someone to be me. I became a woman possessed. Ted, tired of hearing about it, said 'Do it!' So in the summer of 1990, I decided to attend a cookbook-writing seminar given by Marlene Sorosky in Baltimore and invited my friend Barbara Hayford to join me on the six-hundred-mile ride. What a ride it was!"

—*Linda Hegeman*

I was more of a latecomer to bread pudding than Linda. She brought over her favorite one winter morning as a treat for my visiting mother and aunt. It was absolutely delicious; I immediately became a bread pudding fan. When Linda suggested that we go to Baltimore, I innocently went along for the ride and the crab cakes. What a ride it was!"

—*Barbara Hayford*

We left Baltimore as coauthors of a yet-untitled bread pudding cookbook. We now had a realistic approach to cookbook writing and an agent, Linda Hayes. When she called to announce that we had a publisher, to say we became excited is an understatement. Our kitchen counters were soon covered with grocery bags containing bread, eggs, and milk. We filled our refrigerators with bread pudding trials, which sustained us through the writing process. Each morning started with a cup of coffee and bread pudding du jour.

We enlisted an army of friends to attend bread pudding tastings held in our homes. Tasters turned into testers. We traveled from tester to tester, nibbling our way through hundreds of bread puddings.

We met regularly to retest and rewrite recipes, to discard some, and to develop others. Only those recipes that were wonderful survived. This book includes only winners; there's not a dog in the lot.

It took us two and a half years to complete *New-Fangled, Old-Fashioned Bread Puddings*. After millions of bites, we continue to love bread pudding. We consider this collection of recipes an adventure into bread pudding and invite you along for the ride.

Although we do not claim to be food historians, we have traced bread pudding back to Colonial times, finding references to bread pudding pans used by Gulielma Penn, wife of Pennsylvania's founder, and actual recipes for bread puddings in eighteenth- and nineteenth-century cookbooks. Directions to make fine or ordinary bread pudding were found in *The Art of Cookery Made Plain and Easy*, by Hannah Glasse, first published in London in 1796. Several bread pudding recipes appear in Marion Harlin's book, *Common Sense in the Household, a Manual of Practical Housewifery*, published in 1873. We were unable to find any bread puddings included in formal menus during Colonial times and can only surmise that bread puddings were an everyday dish rather than a dressy dessert.

Today bread puddings have attained a status far beyond that of a frugal dessert made with leftover bread and simple ingredients. Was there ever a decline in interest in bread pudding or have they always flourished? We don't know. Is there truly a resurgence of popularity? We think so. It matters little. Bread puddings are here to stay. They are favorites of upscale restaurateurs, caterers, hostesses, and hometown cooks. Bread puddings appeal to nostalgia buffs and trendsetters, foodies, and just plain folks, from Boston to Seattle, from Chicago to New Orleans.

New-Fangled, Old-Fashioned Bread Puddings includes a variety of recipes for every taste and every occasion.

We think of *old-fashioned* bread puddings as those using on-hand basics of stale bread, eggs, milk, and sugar with only raisins and spice thrown in for flair. There are many recipes in this book that our grandmothers would recognize. The puddings of their time comfort us today.

New-fangled bread puddings are innovative combinations of ingredients. Bread puddings can be made any number of ways. Variety and versatility are the keys to the nineties' versions of bread pudding. It's come a long way from its simple origins. Wouldn't Grandma be surprised!

Taking advantage of the creative minds of young chefs across the country, we asked them to share their favorite bread pudding recipes. Their generosity and patience enabled us to adapt their restaurant recipes for home use. Trial and error and many phone calls helped us to reproduce their wonderful creations. Working with the chefs reassured us of our conviction that bread puddings are popular across the nation and that it was time for this book.

New-Fangled, Old-Fashioned Bread Puddings is divided between sweet and savory recipes, each of these sections again divided by bread type. All chocolate recipes are in a section by themselves, regardless of the type of bread used. Included you will find puddings, puffs, stratas, and bread soufflés. Some puddings have a predominance of custard, while others are more dense with a predominance of bread. Some take on a cakelike quality, while others resemble soufflés and puffs in their lightness of taste and texture. Stratas are layered savory bread puddings with the advantage of advance preparation.

We invite you to browse through this book, discovering the many variations of bread puddings. They are all our favorites. If you have never tried bread pudding, start with our first, Sherried Bread Pudding with Citron and Currants (page 54), made with a rich egg bread and smooth custard, studded with candied citron and sherry-soaked currants, crowned with slivered almonds and dusted, ever so lightly, with confectioners' sugar. Need a little love? May we suggest Gingerbread Pudding with Warm Vanilla Butter Sauce (page 63). It's a pudding that brings back memories of a cold day and warm hearts with the scents and tastes of yesterday. Linda's mother loves custard more than bread pudding. Thus our creation in her honor is simply titled Mom's Baked Custard Bread Pudding (page 25). Our nineties' versions include White Chocolate Macadamia Nut Bread Pudding (page 92), a luscious melt-in-your-mouth showstopper, and Apricot Honey Bread Pudding Soufflé with Spa Chocolate Sauce (page 12), a sensual low-fat creation.

For those of you who think of bread pudding as strictly for dessert, you must try Pepper and Wild Mushroom Pizza Bread Pudding (page 102), our irresistible version of gourmet deep-dish pizza. Cheesy goodness and intense southwestern flavors make Black Bean Strata (page 112), our recommendation for contemporary palates. For the unexpected, prepare Pesto Pudding Puff (page 111), pungently flavored with sun-dried tomatoes and basil, puffed with an abundance of provolone and Parmesan cheeses.

We have worked very hard to make sure that each recipe is special and that each one could become your favorite. So try them all.

Joseph Conrad, author of *Lord Jim*, described a cookbook as ". . . the only product of the human mind altogether above suspicion" and said its purpose ". . . can conceivably be no other than to increase the happiness of mankind."

We hope that as you use our book, you will find it so. Here's to you, happiness, and bread pudding.

BREAD PUDDING SECRETS

INGREDIENTS

The primary secret for creating great bread pudding is to use the best and the freshest ingredients you can find. Start with top-quality ingredients and your bread puddings will achieve all-star status in whatever role they play—dessert or entrée.

Bread

In the process of researching this book, we prepared hundreds, if not thousands, of bread puddings. One thing emerged clearly: bread is the key ingredient, and for this reason we've listed it as the first ingredient in every recipe. In any given recipe, the type of bread you use (French, firm-textured white, brioche, and so on), as well as the way you measure the bread, will make a difference. We've tried to be as descriptive as possible so that your results will be similar to ours in taste and texture.

Here are some general guidelines:

- In most cases, use bakery or bakery-quality bread rather than commercial brands. Even if you do not have a favorite local bakery, good-quality bread is not difficult to find. Most supermarkets have in-store bakeries.
- We have used some commercially packaged goods: Pepperidge Farm Original for recipes requiring firm-textured white bread, canned New England brown bread, stuffing (packaged dry mix), tortillas, and ladyfingers.
- Recipes for the homemade breads (Granny's Gingerbread and Cornmeal Poundcake) are provided.

1

- Since the types of French bread and Italian bread found in the United States are similar to each other, their use is interchangeable in the recipes as long as the measurements remain the same in cups and/or ounces. Because the shapes of French and Italian loaves may vary, the number of slices is not an accurate measurement when making substitutions. The preferred bread type, either French or Italian, is listed in the recipe.
- Bread crumbs are made from bakery breads. Never use commercially packaged crumbs.
- Day-old or stale bread is bread that has lost some of its moisture and is firmer, drier, and more crumbly than fresh bread; it is not hard or brittle.
- If you do not have day-old bread, here is a quick way to create stale bread in a matter of minutes. This allows you to make bread pudding on a whim when day-old bread is not on hand.

How to Create "Instant" Stale Bread

Place fresh bread slices, cubes, or crumbs in a 300°F oven until they begin to lose some of their moisture; or leave bread uncovered to air-dry several hours or overnight. Do not over-dry the bread. If you don't wish to use the crusts, remove them before drying the bread; it becomes harder to remove them once the bread is stale.

- Our measurements include the crust unless "crusts removed" is specified.
- Bread crumbs are described according to their size, from fine to coarse. Process bread to desired crumb size.
- In most recipes, we list several measurements for the bread. The first measurement is the most important and accurate; the others are

supporting ones, listed just in case the size and shape of bread that you have is different from what we used in our test kitchen. For example, in Apricot Honey Bread Pudding Soufflé (page 12) the most important measurement is listed first (½-inch cubes to equal 5 generous cups). Use the number (16 to 18) and size (½ inch thick) of slices to guide you. The estimated weight (about 6 ounces) adds further help for accuracy and purchasing.

- An 8-cup Pyrex measuring cup, a ruler, and a kitchen scale are helpful tools for accurate measurement.
- When bread is day-old and you cannot use it immediately to make bread pudding, wrap the bread in plastic wrap and then again in aluminum foil, and freeze it until ready to use. Do not refrigerate bread; this neither preserves freshness nor stales bread.

Eggs

- Use Grade A large eggs except as specified in Shapiro's Danish Bread Pudding with Rum Sauce (page 72).
- Do not taste uncooked egg mixtures because of the potential danger of salmonella poisoning.
- When beating egg whites, use a large, clean, dry bowl. The whites should be at room temperature and free from contaminants and specks of egg yolk. Freeze egg whites left over from rich custard mixtures for future use in Mostly Meringue Bread Pudding Puffs (page 46).
- Some recipes adapt well to the cholesterol-conscious; simply use the substitutions in parentheses.

Milk, Half-and-Half, Cream

- Use whole milk. Use store-bought half-and-half, not a mixture of heavy or whipping cream and milk. Use heavy or whipping cream, not light or coffee cream.
- When whipping cream, use cold heavy or whipping cream, a chilled bowl, and chilled beaters for best results.

- Some recipes adapt well to the cholesterol-conscious; simply use the substitutions in parentheses.

Sugar

- Use the type of white sugar specified in the recipe's ingredient list. Use accurate measurements for granulated and superfine sugar. Some recipes use confectioners' sugar, enough to dust the finished pudding; "enough" is left to your discretion. Dust with confectioners' sugar when the pudding is cool.
- Brown sugar, light and dark, are interchangeable; the preference is specified in the recipe's ingredient list. Use accurate measurements for light and dark brown sugar; always pack brown sugar firmly into a measuring cup.

Cheese

- Grated cheese measurements are in lightly packed cups as well as ounces. Knowing the weight is helpful in purchasing. Be sure to bring goat cheese, Brie cheese, and cream cheese to room temperature before blending with other ingredients.
- Some recipes adapt well to the cholesterol-conscious; simply use the substitutions in parentheses.

Butter

- Most recipes use unsalted butter. Use lightly salted butter only when the ingredient list specifies "butter."
- When a recipe calls for softened butter, bring butter to room temperature. Softened butter is spreadable.
- Some recipes adapt well to the cholesterol-conscious; simply use the substitutions in parentheses.

Chocolate

4   - Use good-quality chocolate such as Lindt; use white chocolate made

from cocoa butter, not palm oil. Use the type of chocolate specified in the recipe's ingredient list unless substitutions are given in Notes.

Vanilla

- Depending upon the recipe, use a whole vanilla bean or pure vanilla extract. Do not use artificial vanilla flavoring.

Spices

- Freshly ground pepper is preferred; use a pepper or spice grinder.
- Freshly grated nutmeg is preferred. Use whole nutmeg and grate on a nutmeg grater or on the small-hole side of an all-purpose grater.
- For optimum flavor, spices should be stored in airtight containers away from light and heat and used within a year after purchase.

Herbs

- When available, fresh herbs are preferred. Dried equivalents are given when substitutions are possible.

Nuts

- Use fresh nuts. Store nuts in airtight containers in the refrigerator or freezer. Some recipes direct you to toast the nuts to enhance their flavor. Follow the instructions specified in the recipe's ingredient list; watch carefully to prevent burning.

PREPARING THE CUSTARD

There are several correct methods for preparing the custard. In some recipes, the liquid is heated before it is added to the eggs or egg mixture. Heating the liquid tempers the eggs, starts the cooking process, and shortens the final cooking time. To achieve the best results with this method, bring the liquid to just under the boiling point. Remove the liquid from the heat when it starts to steam, or when a light film appears on the surface, or when small bubbles appear around the edge. The heated liquid is added gradually to the eggs or egg mixture, whisking or beating continually, until incorporated. If the hot liquid is added all at once, the eggs will curdle. When hot liquid is beaten or whisked into the eggs or egg mixture, foam will develop. Skim and discard foam.

In some recipes the liquid is not heated, but is added directly to the eggs or egg mixture. The additional baking time is calculated into the recipe. In sweet recipes, when eggs and liquid are combined without heating the liquid first, strain the custard through a fine-mesh sieve. This traps any egg particles that were not well mixed. In savory recipes, a smoother custard texture is less important, so straining is not necessary when eggs and liquid are combined without heating the liquid first.

Beating with an electric mixer and whisking with a wire whip are both valid mixing methods. Each recipe states the preferred mixing method; use the alternative method if necessary. When beating with an electric mixer, do not overbeat and whip air into the mixture. When whisking with a wire whip, make sure ingredients are well mixed.

ASSEMBLING THE PUDDING MIXTURE

In some recipes, the bread and other ingredients are placed or layered in the prepared pan or dish before pouring in the custard mixture. In others, the bread, the custard mixture, and other ingredients are tossed together and the entire pudding mixture is poured into the prepared pan or dish. In still others, the bread, the custard mixture, and other ingredients are combined and then finished by folding in stiffly beaten egg whites. Follow the specific directions for assembling in each recipe to achieve the desired result.

STANDING OR WAITING PERIOD

In some recipes, a standing or waiting period is required to allow the bread to absorb the liquid. This step occurs both before and after the pudding mixture is poured into the prepared pan or dish. The standing or waiting period ranges from ten minutes to several hours or overnight. Recipes requiring the longer standing period have the advantage of allowing advance preparation.

BAKING

Use heavy baking pans and dishes; use an oven thermometer to ensure correct oven temperature. If you must change the size of the baking vessel, adjust baking time accordingly. The size and depth of the pan or dish will determine the cooking time—the larger or deeper the pan or dish, the longer the pudding needs to cook.

Some recipes instruct you to set the baking pan or dish in a larger ovenproof pan and to add enough hot water to the pan to come halfway up the sides of the smaller pan or baking dish. This creates a water bath that cradles the custard, protects the eggs from cooking too quickly, and helps the pudding mixture cook evenly from the outside to the center. Recipes with a high ratio of custard to bread are baked in water baths; a water bath is not negotiable for these fragile puddings. Recipes with a high ratio of bread to custard are baked without a water bath.

Because baking times may vary, rely on tests for doneness. In most recipes, a knife is inserted into the pudding one inch from the center. If the knife comes out clean, the pudding is done. The knife is clean when there is no milky substance adhering to it; there may be clear droplets. As an added test for doneness, lightly press the top of the area where the knife was inserted. If liquid oozes out of the knife hole, the pudding is not yet done.

Savory puddings made with grated cheese make the knife test tricky. Any adhering substance may be cheese and not custard; judge carefully.

In some recipes, appearance (a puffed and golden-brown top) and feel (firm to the touch) of the pudding are guides for doneness.

Do not overbake. All puddings continue to cook slightly when removed from the oven.

7

COOLING

When the pudding is done, remove it from the oven and water bath, if used, and place it on a wire rack. Cool for recommended time.

STORING

Let unused portions come to room temperature, cover, and refrigerate. Even refrigerated puddings should not be kept for more than five days.

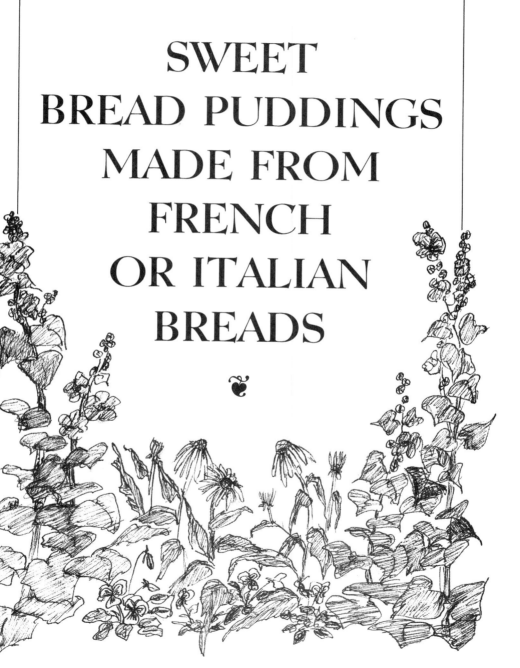

SWEET
BREAD PUDDINGS
MADE FROM
FRENCH
OR ITALIAN
BREADS

My Aunt Leah made the best bread pudding ever. When my eyes barely reached the counter top, I would watch her pour the milk over the bread and help her whip up the eggs. As often as I try to duplicate hers, mine never come out that special. Maybe I haven't layered them with enough warmth, comfort, hugs, and love."

—*Marlene Sorosky*
Author, Dessert Lover's Cookbook

BAROCCO ALIMENTARI'S
❧ BREAD PUDDING

Prepared by Angelica Santos, Pastry Chef, Barocco Alimentari, New York City

Day-old Italian (country) bread, 1 large loaf, crusts removed, cut into ⅜-inch-thick slices

2	**cups milk**
3	**tablespoons granulated sugar**
1	**tablespoon ground cloves**
1½	**cups raisins**
½	**cup dark rum**
6	**large egg yolks**
½	**cup granulated sugar**
2	**cups milk**
1½	**cups heavy or whipping cream**
1½	**teaspoons vanilla extract**
	Ground cinnamon, to taste

NOTES

❏ *A loaf of Barocco's Italian bread weighs 1½ pounds. Once the crusts are removed, the loaf weighs almost 1 pound.*
❏ *This dessert is not too sweet; it can be served for breakfast with warm maple syrup.*

1. Lightly butter a 9- by 13- by 2-inch baking pan.

2. Lay bread flat on trays (not the prepared baking pan).

3. In a small saucepan, warm 2 cups milk together with the 3 tablespoons sugar and cloves. Pour warm milk mixture over all bread slices. Set aside.

4. Stir together raisins and rum and set aside to soak.

5. In a large bowl and with an electric mixer set at low speed, beat together egg yolks, the ½ cup sugar, 2 cups milk, heavy cream, vanilla, and a dash of cinnamon.

6. Preheat oven to 350°F.

7. Gently squeeze excess milk out of bread. Cover bottom of prepared dish with a layer of soaked bread. Spoon on half the raisins and sprinkle with cinnamon to taste. Pour one third of the cream mixture over this layer. Repeat with second layer of bread, the second half of the raisins, cinnamon to taste, and another third of the cream mixture. Finish with the third layer of bread and the last third of the cream, omitting raisins and cinnamon for the top.

8. Bake until golden brown, about 50 minutes.

9. Remove from oven onto a wire rack.

10. Cut into squares. Serve warm or at room temperature with warm zabaglione.

Let unused portions come to room temperature, cover, and refrigerate.

YIELD: *6 to 8 servings*

APRICOT HONEY BREAD PUDDING SOUFFLÉ ❦ WITH SPA CHOCOLATE SAUCE

This light and luscious low-fat soufflé has beautiful color and heavenly taste. Drizzle with Spa Chocolate Sauce with no guilt feelings.

Day-old French bread, cut into ½-inch cubes to equal 5 generous cups, 16 to 18 ½-inch-thick slices, about 6 ounces

½	cup dried apricots, 16 to 18 halves
1½	cups apricot nectar
½	cup orange blossom honey
1	tablespoon fresh lemon juice
	Grated zest of 1 lemon
2	large eggs
1½	cups low-fat milk
¼	cup granulated sugar
1	tablespoon vanilla extract
1	tablespoon brandy
4	large egg whites
	Pinch of salt
3	tablespoons granulated sugar, divided
	Spa Chocolate Sauce, 1 cup (recipe follows)

1. Generously butter bottom of a 1½-quart soufflé dish.

2. In a small heavy saucepan, combine apricots, nectar, honey, lemon juice, and zest. Over medium heat, bring to a simmer and cook until apricots are soft, 10 to 15 minutes. With a slotted spoon, remove apricots. When cool enough to handle, chop apricots coarsely and set aside.

3. Increase heat to medium-high and reduce apricot liquid to 1⅓ cups, 5 to 10 minutes. Remove from heat and cool slightly.

4. In a large bowl, whisk eggs. Add milk, the ¼ cup sugar, vanilla, brandy, and apricot liquid and whisk until well mixed.

5. Add bread cubes and chopped apricots to custard mixture; with a spoon, toss to combine. Let stand for 30 minutes so that the bread absorbs the liquid.

6. Preheat oven to 350°F.

7. In a clean, dry, large bowl, and with an electric mixer set on medium-low speed, beat egg whites and salt until foamy. Increase mixer speed to medium-high and gradually add all but 1 teaspoon of the 3 tablespoons sugar, beating continuously until stiff but not dry.

NOTES

❑ *If you do not have day-old bread, place fresh bread in a 300°F oven until it begins to lose some of its moisture, or leave fresh bread uncovered to air-dry for several hours or overnight.*
❑ *Expect the bread soufflé to fall as it cools.*
❑ *Soufflé connoisseurs may prefer to undercook the pudding slightly for a creamier texture.*
❑ *Most honeys may be substituted for the preferred orange blossom honey.*

Gently fold whites into pudding mixture.

8. Pour pudding mixture into prepared dish. Sprinkle top with the remaining teaspoon sugar.

9. Bake for 45 to 50 minutes, or until custard is set (knife inserted 1 inch from center comes out clean), pudding is puffed, and top is golden brown.

10. Remove from oven onto a wire rack and cool for at least 10 minutes.

11. Spoon onto serving plates. Serve warm with Spa Chocolate Sauce (recipe follows), 1 to 2 tablespoons sauce for each serving, or low-fat vanilla yogurt.

Let unused portions come to room temperature, cover, and refrigerate.

YIELD: *6 servings*

Spa Chocolate Sauce

Prepared by Steven Keneipp, Chef-Proprietor, The Classic Kitchen, Noblesville, Indiana

1   cup frozen apple juice concentrate, thawed
1   cup orange blossom honey
2   cups imported or Dutch-processed cocoa
¾   cup water
2   tablespoons vanilla extract

1. In a small heavy saucepan over medium heat, bring apple juice concentrate and honey to a simmer.

2. With a whisk, gradually stir in cocoa, beating until mixture is smooth.

3. Whisk in water. Remove from heat and stir in vanilla.

4. Spoon sauce into a glass container and refrigerate until ready to use.

YIELD: *3 cups*

NOTES

❑ *Use a Dutch-processed or imported cocoa; otherwise, the sauce will be too bitter.*
❑ *Because the sauce is intense in flavor, add a drizzle of sauce, rather than a glob.*
❑ *Substitute brandy, orange liqueur, or rum for part of the water.*
❑ *This recipe was tested using a third of the listed ingredients to yield 1 cup sauce, more than enough for 6 servings of Apricot Honey Bread Pudding Soufflé.*

13

BIBA'S HOT CARAMEL
❦ BREAD PUDDING

Prepared by Kilian B. Weigand, Pastry Chef, Biba, Boston

"Whenever this pudding is on the menu, it serves as my breakfast. Cold from the refrigerator, with a large, very strong, unsweetened cup of black coffee. Yum. Bread pudding isn't just for dessert anymore."

Day-old French baguette, 20 ¾-inch-thick slices, cut into ¾-inch cubes to equal 9 to 10 cups, about 10 ounces

¼	cup currants
⅓	cup dark rum
2	cups granulated sugar
½	cup water
⅛	teaspoon cream of tartar
4	cups milk
1	cup heavy or whipping cream
1	cup granulated sugar
½	teaspoon salt
8	large egg yolks
1	tablespoon vanilla extract
4	large egg whites

Crème fraîche, enough to drizzle over finished pudding

NOTES

❑ *Brioche may be substituted for the French bread.*

❑ *What makes this unusual is the combination of three separate layers in the pudding. The bottom layer is a strong, sweet caramel. The center is a layer of rich custard-soaked cubes of bread, and the top is a layer of browned, creamy egg whites.*

1. Butter a 9- by 13- by 2-inch baking pan.

2. Soak currants in rum for at least 30 minutes.

3. In a small heavy saucepan, combine the 2 cups sugar, water, and cream of tartar. Over medium-low heat, swirl until sugar dissolves. Increase heat to medium-high and continue cooking, without stirring, until syrup is a deep golden brown, 12 to 15 minutes. Immediately pour caramel syrup into prepared pan, turning rapidly to coat bottom.

4. Sprinkle caramel with currants and rum. Set aside.

5. In a medium-size heavy saucepan, bring milk, cream, the 1 cup sugar, and salt almost to a boil.

6. In a large bowl and with an electric mixer, beat egg yolks. Gradually add milk mixture, beating continually until incorporated. Add vanilla; stir. Cool slightly.

7. In a separate large bowl, beat egg whites until stiff. Gently fold whites into custard mixture.

8. Preheat oven to 350°F.

9. Place bread in a very large bowl. Pour custard mixture over bread and, with a spoon, toss to combine. Let stand for 10 minutes so that the bread absorbs the liquid.

10. Pour pudding mixture into prepared pan. Set pan in a larger ovenproof pan and add enough hot water to come halfway up sides of smaller pan.

11. Bake for 45 minutes, or until custard is set (knife inserted 1 inch from center comes out clean), pudding is puffed, and top is golden brown.

12. Remove from water bath onto a wire rack and cool for 10 minutes.

13. Spoon a liberal amount of the pudding into a serving bowl, making sure you do not forget a little extra of the caramel. Serve warm with a small spoonful of crème fraîche drizzled over the top.

Let unused portions come to room temperature, cover, and refrigerate.

YIELD: *12 servings*

BUTTERSCOTCH
❦ BREAD PUDDING

A butterscotch brownie topped with rich, gooey caramel sauce makes this an ultra-rich treat. A small portion satisfies any sweet tooth.

Day-old French bread, 12 ounces, crusts removed, 32 to 36 ½-inch-thick slices

NOTES

❏ *If you do not have day-old bread, place fresh bread in a 300°F oven until it begins to lose some of its moisture, or leave fresh bread uncovered to air-dry for several hours or overnight.*
❏ *Pudding may appear to be underdone after 45 minutes of baking due to caramel topping. Do not overbake; pudding will become firmer as it cools.*
❏ *Leave crusts on bread slices for a denser pudding.*

1   12-ounce package butterscotch chips
4   tablespoons butter, softened
1¾ cups firmly packed light brown sugar
4   large eggs
2   cups heavy or whipping cream
2   cups milk
1   teaspoon vanilla extract

T O P P I N G

1   14-ounce package caramels
1   5½-ounce can evaporated milk
1   cup chopped pecans, toasted in a 350°F oven for 7 to 10 minutes

1. Generously butter a 9- by 13- by 2-inch baking pan.

2. Arrange bread slices in prepared dish in an overlapping pattern, fallen-domino fashion. Sprinkle butterscotch chips evenly over bread slices, tucking at least half the chips in between slices.

3. In a large bowl and with an electric mixer set at medium-low speed, cream butter and brown sugar until smooth. Increase mixer speed to medium and add eggs, one at a time, beating just to blend after each addition. Add cream, milk, and vanilla; continue beating until well mixed.

4. Carefully pour custard mixture over bread. Cover with plastic wrap and press down with your hands or back of a spoon so that the bread absorbs the liquid. Let stand for 30 minutes. (At this point, pudding mixture can be refrigerated several hours or overnight.)

5. Preheat oven to 350°F.

6. Remove plastic wrap from pudding. Bake for 30 minutes.

7. Meanwhile, prepare topping. In the top of a double boiler over simmering water, heat caramels and evaporated milk until caramels are melted and mixture is smooth, 15 to 20 minutes. Stir occasionally. Remove entire double boiler from heat; keep warm.

8. After baking for 30 minutes, remove pudding from oven.

Pour caramel mixture evenly over pudding and sprinkle top with pecans. Continue baking for an additional 15 minutes.

9. Remove from oven onto a wire rack and cool for at least 30 minutes.

10. Cut into squares. Serve warm or at room temperature. Add a scoop of ice cream just for fun.

Let unused portions come to room temperature, cover, and refrigerate.

YIELD: *15 servings*

CREAMY BREAD
❧ PUDDING

Prepared by Johanne Killeen and George Germon, Chefs-Proprietors, Al Forno, Providence. From *Cucina Simpatica* by Johanne Killeen and George Germon. Copyright © 1991 by Johanne Killeen and George Germon. Reprinted by permission of HarperCollins Publishers Inc.

"Bread pudding is comfort food. At its best it is sublime. We prefer bread pudding with a high ratio of custard—silky smooth, rich custard to contrast with the coarse texture of bread."

Country bread, 10 ⅜-inch-thick slices, crusts removed

1	**vanilla bean**
6	**cups heavy or whipping cream**
8	**large eggs**
1½	**cups granulated sugar**

NOTES

❑ *The recipe may be halved.*
❑ *Portuguese sweet bread is a good choice for this pudding, as is any fine-crumbed bread or cake.*
❑ *Baking time may increase slightly due to oven being opened every 5 minutes to stir custard.*

1. Set aside twelve 1-cup soufflé ramekins.

2. Split vanilla bean in half lengthwise with a paring knife. Scrape seeds from pod. In a heavy saucepan, combine seeds, pod, and cream.

3. Bring cream almost to a boil, remove from heat, and set aside, uncovered, for 1 hour to steep.

4. Preheat oven to 300°F.

5. Strain cream through a fine-mesh sieve, discarding pod, and reheat almost to a boil.

6. In a large bowl, whisk eggs with sugar. Very slowly add hot cream to eggs, whisking constantly.

7. Divide bread slices evenly among ramekins. Pour custard mixture over bread, submerging slices with a spoon so that they soak up some of the liquid.

8. Place ramekins in a roasting pan. Add enough hot water to the pan to come halfway up sides of ramekins.

9. Bake for 30 to 40 minutes, until edges have set and center is still a bit runny. The pudding will continue to cook out of the oven and will set completely as it cools. For a smooth, creamy texture, stir pudding every 5 minutes during baking: run a rubber scraper around inside of ramekins, gently pushing outside of pudding toward the center. The pudding will cook evenly and the custard will be silky smooth.

10. Remove from water bath onto a wire rack and cool for 10 minutes.

11. Serve warm in the ramekins.

Let unused portions come to room temperature, cover, and refrigerate.

YIELD: *12 servings*

CRÈME CARAMEL PUMPKIN
❦ BREAD PUDDING

Prepared by Peggy A. Elliott, Pastry Chef, Tulio, Seattle, and Peggy M. Elliott, her mother, at home, St. Paul

"It's pretty tough competition to replace a loved traditional item from the Thanksgiving table, but my mother adapted mine and has used this one for a few years now in feeding her crowd of thirty—and I believe they approve."

—Peggy A. Elliott

Day-old French bread, crusts removed, cut into ½-inch cubes to equal 6 cups, approximately 27 ½-inch-thick slices, about 9 to 10 ounces with crusts

8	tablespoons unsalted butter
1	teaspoon ground cinnamon
1	teaspoon ground ginger
½	teaspoon grated nutmeg
¼	teaspoon ground cloves

CARAMEL

2	cups granulated sugar
6	tablespoons water
2	teaspoons fresh lemon juice
	Heavy or whipping cream, enough to thin caramel, about ½ cup
1 to 2	Rome apples

CUSTARD

5	large eggs
1½	cups granulated sugar
2	cups canned pumpkin
1½	cups half-and-half
1	tablespoon vanilla extract
½	teaspoon salt
1	teaspoon ground cinnamon
1	teaspoon ground ginger
½	teaspoon grated nutmeg
¼	teaspoon ground cloves
¼	teaspoon ground allspice
⅛	teaspoon freshly ground black pepper

1. Generously butter a 9- by 2-inch round cake pan.

2. In a small heavy saucepan, melt butter with cinnamon, ginger, nutmeg, and cloves. Place bread cubes in a large bowl. Add butter mixture; with a spoon, toss to coat.

3. Prepare caramel. In a large skillet, place the 2 cups sugar, water, and lemon juice. Over medium-low heat, swirl until sugar dissolves. Increase heat to medium-high and continue cooking, without stirring, until syrup is a light golden brown. Immediately pour a ¼-inch-thick layer of caramel into prepared pan, saving some for caramel sauce.

4. Return skillet to heat and whisk in enough cream to form a thin sauce. Cook an additional few minutes to reduce to desired consistency. Bring caramel sauce to room temperature and refrigerate until ready to use. When needed, reheat in the top of a double boiler.

5. Peel and core apples. Cut into ½-inch cubes to equal 1½ cups and press cubes into caramel in prepared pan. Place bread mixture on top of caramel and apples.

6. Prepare custard. In a separate large bowl and with an electric mixer set on medium speed, beat together eggs and the 1½ cups sugar. Reduce mixer speed to low and add pumpkin, half-and-half, vanilla, salt, cinnamon, ginger, nutmeg, cloves, allspice, and pepper; continue beating until well mixed.

7. Carefully pour some custard mixture over bread. Let settle; add remaining custard mixture. Let stand for 1 hour so that the bread absorbs the liquid.

8. Preheat oven to 350°F.

9. Set pan in a larger ovenproof pan. Add enough hot water to the pan to come halfway up sides of smaller pan.

10. Bake for 50 to 60 minutes, or until custard is set (knife inserted 1 inch from center comes out clean) and pudding is firm to the touch.

11. Remove from water bath onto a wire rack and cool to room temperature. Refrigerate several hours or overnight.

12. When ready to serve, set cake pan in a larger pan. Add hot water and let stand for a few minutes to soften caramel. Run a knife around inside rim of pan and carefully invert onto a serving platter. Cut into wedges and serve chilled or at room temperature with caramel sauce.

Let unused portions come to room temperature, cover, and refrigerate.

YIELD: *10 servings*

NOTES

❑ *Cooked, puréed acorn or butternut squash may be substituted for pumpkin.*

❑ *This recipe was successfully tested with 4 cups of bread cubes. The pudding had a more custardlike texture.*

❑ *Peggy and Peggy caramelize their sugar using the dry method. In this method, sugar is melted directly in a heavy skillet; no liquid is used. It can be very tricky.*

❑ *There may be a small amount of pumpkin custard mixture that will not fit into prepared pan. Fill a custard cup and bake alongside cake pan. The individual pudding will bake in 30 to 40 minutes; the knife test is valid here.*

❑ *We like Mary's Apple Sabayon (page 35) with this.*

CRUNCHY APPLE
❦ BREAD PUDDING

This dessert strata is really a gourmet apple crisp—perfect for Sunday suppers. Tart Granny Smith apple chunks, golden raisins, and bits of cream cheese are topped with a sweet walnut crunch.

Day-old French bread, 9 1-inch-thick slices, about 7 ounces

1	cup firmly packed light brown sugar
¾	cup water
2	tablespoons dry sherry
1	teaspoon aniseed
2	whole cloves
1	cinnamon stick
9	tablespoons unsalted butter
1	large Granny Smith apple
⅔	cup coarsely chopped walnuts
¼	cup golden raisins
4	ounces cream cheese, cut into 1-inch cubes
⅓	cup finely chopped walnuts
3	tablespoons granulated sugar
1	teaspoon ground cinnamon
2	tablespoons unsalted butter, melted

NOTE

❑ *If you do not have day-old bread, place fresh bread in 300°F oven until it begins to lose some of its moisture, or leave fresh bread uncovered to air-dry for several hours or overnight.*

1. Lightly butter a 1½-quart soufflé or deep-sided baking dish.

2. In a small heavy saucepan, combine brown sugar, water, sherry, aniseed, cloves, and cinnamon stick. Bring to a boil over medium-high heat, stirring occasionally. Boil 30 seconds. Remove from heat and, with a fine-mesh sieve, strain into a bowl. Discard aniseed, cloves, and cinnamon stick and set liquid aside.

3. In a large skillet over medium heat, melt 6 tablespoons of the 9 tablespoons butter. Add bread slices in batches and sauté on both sides until bread is browned. Add the remaining 3 tablespoons butter as needed. Remove bread slices from skillet and set aside.

4. Preheat oven to 350°F.

5. Peel and core apple; cut into ½-inch cubes. In a medium bowl, combine apple, the ⅔ cup walnuts, raisins, and cream cheese.

6. Place 4 bread slices in bottom of prepared dish. Add fruit mixture. Top with the remaining bread slices. Slowly pour brown sugar syrup evenly over bread slices so that the bread absorbs the liquid.

7. In a small bowl, combine the ⅓ cup walnuts, granulated sugar, and cinnamon. Sprinkle top with nut mixture.

8. Bake for 25 minutes. Drizzle top with the 2 tablespoons melted butter. Bake for 5 more minutes. Turn oven off; let pudding stand in oven for an additional 15 minutes.

9. Remove from oven onto a wire rack and cool for at least 10 minutes.

10. Spoon onto serving plates. Serve warm or at room temperature.

Let unused portions come to room temperature, cover, and refrigerate.

YIELD: *6 servings*

EGGNOG CUSTARD
❦ BREAD PUDDING

Celebrate the holidays with this velvety cup of cheer. Our rich rum-and brandy-flavored custard combines with a delicate French bread crust and is dusted, ever so gently, with the fragrance of ground nutmeg.

Day-old French bread, 6 ⅓-inch-thick slices, about 1 ounce

¼	cup finely chopped candied fruit
2	cups heavy or whipping cream
½	cup milk
5	large egg yolks
1	large egg
½	cup granulated sugar
1	teaspoon vanilla extract
½	teaspoon rum extract
½	teaspoon brandy extract
½	to 1 teaspoon grated nutmeg, divided

NOTES

❏ *If you do not have day-old bread, place fresh bread in a 300°F oven until it begins to lose some of its moisture, or leave fresh bread uncovered to air-dry for several hours or overnight.*
❏ *Leftover fruitcake? One to two 1-inch fruitcake cubes may be substituted for the bread slice in each cup. Eliminate candied fruit.*

1. Lightly butter six 5-ounce ceramic custard cups. Preheat oven to 350°F.

2. Place a bread slice in each prepared cup. Scatter candied fruit evenly over bread slices. Set aside.

3. In a small heavy saucepan over medium heat, bring cream and milk almost to a boil.

4. In a large bowl and with an electric mixer set on medium speed, beat together egg yolks, egg, sugar, extracts, and ½ teaspoon nutmeg. Gradually add cream mixture, beating continually until incorporated. Skim and discard foam.

5. Pour custard mixture evenly over bread slices. Sprinkle tops with the remaining nutmeg.

6. Set cups in an ovenproof pan just large enough to hold them snugly. Add enough hot water to the pan to come halfway up sides of cups.

7. Bake for 30 to 35 minutes, or until custard is set (knife inserted off center comes out clean) and tops are lightly browned. Do not overcook.

8. Remove from water bath onto a wire rack and cool for at least 10 minutes.

9. Serve in the cups, warm or chilled.

Let unused portions come to room temperature, cover, and refrigerate.

YIELD: *6 servings*

MOM'S BAKED CUSTARD
❦ BREAD PUDDING

This homey dessert speaks to those who love custard and real comfort food. It is simple to make and simply wonderful.

Day-old French bread, 6 ¼-inch-thick slices, cut into halves, about ¾ ounce

2	**cups milk**
½	**cup heavy or whipping cream**
5	**large egg yolks**
1	**large egg**
½	**cup granulated sugar**
1	**teaspoon vanilla extract**
⅛	**teaspoon salt**
	Grated nutmeg, enough to sprinkle on top of puddings

NOTE

❏ *If you do not have day-old bread, place fresh bread in a 300°F oven until it begins to lose some of its moisture, or leave fresh bread uncovered to air-dry for several hours or overnight.*

1. Lightly butter four 1-cup soufflé ramekins. Preheat oven to 350°F.

2. Divide bread halves equally among prepared ramekins. Set aside.

3. In a small heavy saucepan, bring milk and cream almost to a boil over medium heat.

4. In a large bowl and with an electric mixer set on medium speed, beat together egg yolks, egg, sugar, vanilla, and salt. Gradually add milk mixture, beating continually until incorporated. Skim and discard foam.

5. Pour custard mixture evenly over bread slices. Sprinkle tops with nutmeg.

6. Set ramekins in an ovenproof pan just large enough to hold them snugly. Add enough hot water to the pan to come halfway up sides of ramekins.

7. Bake for 25 to 30 minutes, or until custard is set (knife inserted off center comes out clean). Do not overcook.

8. Remove from water bath onto a rack and cool for at least 10 minutes.

9. Serve in the ramekins, warm or chilled.

Let unused portions come to room temperature, cover, and refrigerate.

YIELD: *4 servings*

FIGGY BREAD PUDDING
❦ WITH BRANDY HARD SAUCE

The ancient Christmas carol urges: "So bring us a figgy pudding and bring it right here." This figgy pudding answers with a brandy custard loaded with plumped fig slices. Brandy Hard Sauce melts over the warm pudding, releasing memorable scents of allspice and cinnamon.

Day-old Italian bread, 8 ounces, approximately 12 ½-inch-thick slices

12 tablespoons unsalted butter, melted
1⅓ cups heavy or whipping cream
1⅓ cups milk
1 8-ounce package dried Mission figs, hard stems removed, thinly sliced or diced, 1½ cups
3 large eggs
3 large egg yolks
⅔ cup firmly packed light brown sugar
2 teaspoons vanilla extract
½ teaspoon ground allspice
½ teaspoon ground cinnamon
⅓ cup brandy
¾ cup chopped walnuts, toasted in a 350° F oven for 7 to 10 minutes
  Brandy Hard Sauce (recipe follows)

1. Lightly butter a 2½-quart shallow baking dish.

2. Brush both sides of bread slices with the melted butter and cut into 1-inch strips. Set aside.

3. In a medium-size heavy saucepan, combine cream, milk, and fig pieces. Over medium heat, bring mixture almost to a boil. Remove from heat, cover, and let stand for 30 minutes.

4. In a large bowl and with an electric mixer set on medium speed, beat eggs, yolks, and brown sugar until combined and mixture is smooth.

5. With a fine-mesh sieve, strain cream mixture into bowl with eggs and sugar, reserving fig pieces. Add vanilla, allspice, cinnamon, and brandy and beat until well mixed.

6. Arrange half the bread strips in prepared dish. Sprinkle half the fig pieces and half the walnuts over bread. Repeat layering.

7. Carefully pour custard mixture over bread. Cover with plastic wrap and press down with your hands or back of a spoon so that the bread absorbs the liquid. Let stand for 30 minutes.

8. Preheat oven to 350°F.

9. Remove plastic wrap from pudding. Set baking dish in a larger ovenproof pan. Add enough hot water to the pan to come halfway up sides of baking dish.

10. Bake for 45 minutes, or until custard is set (knife inserted 1 inch from center comes out clean), pudding is puffed, and top is browned.

11. Remove from water bath onto a wire rack and cool for at least 10 minutes.

12. Spoon onto serving plates. Serve warm with Brandy Hard Sauce (recipe follows), 2 tablespoons sauce for each serving.

Let unused portions come to room temperature, cover, and refrigerate.

YIELD: *10 servings*

Brandy Hard Sauce

12 **tablespoons butter, softened**
2¼ **cups confectioners' sugar**
3 **tablespoons brandy**
1 **teaspoon vanilla extract**

1. In a large bowl and with an electric mixer set on medium speed, beat butter until light and fluffy.

2. Reduce mixer speed to medium-low. Gradually add confectioners' sugar, brandy, and vanilla, beating until creamy.

3. Refrigerate until ready to use. Bring to room temperature to serve.

YIELD: *Scant 1½ cups*

GRANOLA CRUMBLE
❦ BREAD PUDDING

Where's the bread? This pudding tastes more like a fruit compote. Large chunks of apples and pears, along with chopped dates, are baked in the oven. Honey-sweetened granola is folded in at the end to make a low-fat dessert with no compromise in taste. Perfect for family and casual entertaining.

Day-old French bread, cut into ½-inch cubes to equal 4 cups, 13 to 15 ½-inch-thick slices, about 5 ounces

1⅓	cups apple juice
1	cup firmly packed light brown sugar
2	whole cloves
1	cinnamon stick
5	whole black peppercorns
1	tablespoon fresh lemon juice
2	large Granny Smith apples
1	large, firm Red Bartlett pear
½	cup chopped dates
3	tablespoons granulated sugar
½	teaspoon ground allspice
1	cup Low-Fat Granola, (recipe follows), divided

NOTES

❑ *If you do not have day-old bread, place fresh bread in a 300°F oven until it begins to lose some of its moisture, or leave fresh bread uncovered to air-dry for several hours or overnight.*
❑ *Store-bought, low-fat granola may be substituted for Low-Fat Granola (recipe follows).*
❑ *Brown sugar may be reduced to ¾ cup.*

1. Coat a 1¾-quart soufflé or deep-sided baking dish with non-stick vegetable spray.

2. In a small heavy saucepan, combine apple juice, brown sugar, cloves, cinnamon stick, peppercorns, and lemon juice. Bring to a boil over medium-high heat. Continue to boil until reduced to 1½ cups, 10 to 15 minutes. Remove from heat and, with a fine-mesh sieve, strain. Discard cloves, peppercorns, and cinnamon stick and set liquid aside.

3. Preheat oven to 375°F.

4. Peel and core apples and pear. Slice fruit lengthwise into ½-inch-thick slices and then in half crosswise.

5. In prepared dish, combine apples, pears, dates, granulated sugar, and allspice. Top with bread cubes. Slowly pour apple juice syrup evenly over bread cubes so that the bread absorbs the liquid.

6. Cover with aluminum foil and bake for 20 minutes. Uncover and stir. Bake for 5 more minutes. Stir; top with half the granola and bake for an additional 5 minutes.

7. Remove from oven onto a wire rack and cool for at least 10 minutes.

8. Spoon into serving bowls. Serve warm or at room temperature with yogurt and the remaining granola.

Let unused portions come to room temperature, cover, and refrigerate.

YIELD: *6 servings*

Low-Fat Granola

2	**tablespoons honey**
¼	**teaspoon salt**
½	**teaspoon vanilla extract**
1	**cup old-fashioned (not instant) rolled oats**
1	**cup thick rolled wheat flakes (health food product)**
1	**cup chopped walnuts**

1. Coat a 15- by 10-inch jelly roll pan with nonstick vegetable spray. Preheat oven to 325°F.

2. In a medium saucepan, combine honey and salt. Heat until warm. Remove from heat and stir in vanilla.

3. Add oats, wheat flakes, and walnuts; stir to coat.

4. Spread mixture in an even layer on prepared pan.

5. Bake for 13 to 15 minutes, or until golden brown, stirring twice during baking.

6. Remove from oven and cool.

Unused portion should be stored in an airtight container.

YIELD: *3 cups*

NOTE

❑ *One third of this recipe is needed for Granola Crumble Bread Pudding.*

JANE ANNE'S ORANGE
❦ BREAD PUDDING SOUFFLÉ

Whip up this heavenly dish, a new-fangled version of a Grand Marnier soufflé, whenever you need a light finish to a rich meal.

Day-old French bread, crusts removed, cut into ½-inch cubes to equal 2 cups, 8 to 9 ½-inch-thick slices, about 3 ounces with crusts

NOTES

❑ *If you do not have day-old bread, place fresh bread in 300°F oven until it begins to lose some of its moisture, or leave fresh bread uncovered to air-dry for several hours or overnight.*
❑ *Expect the bread soufflé to fall as it cools.*

⅔	**cup granulated sugar**
1	**teaspoon grated nutmeg**
	Grated zest of 1 lemon
2	**tablespoons fresh lemon juice**
	Grated zest of 1 orange
¼	**cup fresh orange juice**
¼	**cup Grand Marnier or other orange-flavored liqueur**
1	**teaspoon vanilla extract**
8	**tablespoons unsalted butter, melted and cooled slightly**
4	**large eggs, separated**
¼	**cup milk**
	Pinch of salt

1. Generously butter bottom of a 1½-quart soufflé dish.

2. In a large bowl, mix together sugar, nutmeg, lemon zest, lemon juice, orange zest, orange juice, Grand Marnier, vanilla, and melted butter. Add bread cubes and toss to coat.

3. Preheat oven to 325°F.

4. In a separate large bowl and with an electric mixer set on medium-high speed, beat egg yolks until thick and lemon colored, 5 minutes. Gradually add milk, beating continually until incorporated. Pour over bread mixture and stir gently. Set aside.

5. In a clean, dry, large bowl and with an electric mixer set on medium-low speed, beat egg whites and salt until foamy. Increase mixer speed to medium-high, beating continuously until stiff but not dry. Gently fold whites into pudding mixture.

6. Pour pudding mixture into prepared dish. Set dish in a larger ovenproof pan. Add enough hot water to the pan to come halfway up sides of baking dish.

7. Bake for 50 minutes, or until custard is set (knife inserted 1 inch from center comes out clean), pudding is puffed, and top is golden brown.

8. Remove from water bath onto a wire rack and cool for at least 10 minutes.

9. Spoon onto serving plates. Serve warm, at room temperature, or chilled.

Let unused portions come to room temperature, cover, and refrigerate.

YIELD: *6 servings*

PEAR AND CRANBERRY BREAD PUDDING
❦ WITH CARAMEL SAUCE

Prepared by Dawn Bailey, Pastry Chef, John Ash & Co., Santa Rosa, California

French bread, approximately 40 ⅛-inch-thick slices

1½ cups dried cranberries
1½ cups chopped dried pears
3　cups half-and-half
⅓　cup granulated sugar
2　large eggs
½　teaspoon ground allspice

T O P P I N G

6　large eggs, separated
¼　cup granulated sugar, divided
　Caramel Sauce (recipe follows)

NOTES

❑ *To slice bread thin, freeze bread, defrost slightly, and slice.*
❑ *Fill each ramekin with a scant ⅓ cup custard and ½ cup egg topping.*

1. Butter ten 1-cup soufflé ramekins. Line each ramekin with bread slices, both bottom and sides, trimming bread to fit perfectly. No bread should extend above sides.

2. Combine dried fruits and divide them equally among ramekins, placing fruit on the bread.

3. In a large bowl, whisk half-and-half, the ⅓ cup sugar, the 2 eggs, and allspice. Pour custard mixture onto bread and fruit.

4. Preheat oven to 350°F.

5. In a clean, dry, large bowl, whip the 6 egg whites until soft peaks form. Gradually add 2 tablespoons of the ¼ cup sugar and whip a little longer. Add yolks, one at a time; whip until fairly stiff.

6. Spoon egg topping over each pudding and spread to cover fruit. Sprinkle with the remaining sugar.

7. Bake for 30 minutes, or until topping is golden.

8. Remove from oven onto a rack and cool slightly.

9. Run a knife around inside rim of each ramekin and carefully unmold onto a plate. Invert again onto a serving plate so that the top of the pudding is facing up. Serve warm or at room temperature with warm Caramel Sauce (recipe follows).

Let unused portions come to room temperature, cover, and refrigerate.

YIELD: *10 servings*

Caramel Sauce

Prepared by Dawn Bailey

1   cup heavy or whipping cream
1¾ cups granulated sugar
¾   cup water
5   tablespoons unsalted butter
1   teaspoon vanilla extract
    Pinch of salt
2   tablespoons rum or brandy (optional)

1. Heat cream so it is too hot to touch; set aside.

2. Combine sugar and water in a saucepan and bring to a boil. Do not stir once mixture comes to a boil. With a pastry brush, wash down sides of pan with water to get rid of any sugar crystals.

3. When sugar mixture becomes a light golden color, take pan off heat and whisk in hot cream. Be careful; mixture will bubble and is extremely hot.

4. Pour mixture into a bowl. Do not scrape sides of pan; leave any sugar crystals on pan and not in sauce.

5. Add butter, a tablespoon at a time, then vanilla, salt, and rum or brandy.

6. Serve warm.

This sauce keeps well in the refrigerator for up to 10 days and can be reheated.

YIELD: *2 cups*

PERSIMMON BREAD PUDDING
❦ WITH MARY'S APPLE SABAYON

An autumn or winter dessert, this moist cakelike pudding features a subtle pumpkin flavor, enhanced with ginger, nutmeg, and cloves. Several sauces give it versatility.

Day-old Italian bread, processed into medium-coarse crumbs to equal 2 cups, 3 to 4 ½-inch-thick slices

5	tablespoons unsalted butter, softened
½	cup granulated sugar
½	cup firmly packed dark brown sugar
2	large eggs
½	teaspoon baking soda
¼	teaspoon salt
1	teaspoon ground cinnamon
¼	teaspoon ground cloves
½	teaspoon grated nutmeg
½	teaspoon ground ginger
1	5-ounce can evaporated milk
1	cup persimmon pulp
½	cup chopped pecans, toasted in a 350°F oven for 7 to 10 minutes

Mary's Apple Sabayon (recipe follows), 2 cups

NOTES

❏ *If you do not have day-old bread, place fresh bread in a 300°F oven until it begins to lose some of its moisture, or leave fresh bread uncovered to air-dry for several hours or overnight.*
❏ *Canned pumpkin may be substituted for the persimmon pulp. Increase ground cloves to ½ teaspoon.*

1. Generously butter an 8-inch square baking pan. Preheat oven to 350°F.

2. In a large bowl and with an electric mixer set on medium speed, cream butter, granulated sugar, and brown sugar until smooth. Add eggs, one at a time, beating just to blend after each addition. Add baking soda, salt, cinnamon, cloves, nutmeg, and ginger. Beat just to blend. Add evaporated milk; continue beating until well mixed.

3. Add bread crumbs, persimmon pulp, and pecans; stir until well mixed.

4. Pour pudding mixture into prepared pan. Cover with aluminum foil.

5. Bake for 30 minutes. Uncover and bake for an additional 15 minutes, or until pudding is set (toothpick inserted comes out clean). Do not overbake.

6. Remove from oven onto a wire rack and cool for at least 15 minutes.

7. Cut into squares. Serve warm or at room temperature with Mary's Apple Sabayon (recipe follows), scant ¼ cup sauce for each serving; Warm Vanilla Butter Sauce (page 65), 2 generous tablespoons for each serving; or Brandy Hard Sauce (page 27), 2 tablespoons sauce for each serving.

Let unused portions come to room temperature, cover, and refrigerate.

YIELD: *9 servings*

Mary's Apple Sabayon

4   **large egg yolks**
⅓   **cup granulated sugar**
½   **cup plus 2 tablespoons apple juice concentrate**
2   **tablespoons applejack**
1½   **cups heavy or whipping cream**

1. In a medium-size stainless-steel bowl, whisk egg yolks and sugar until sugar dissolves and mixture is lemon colored, 5 minutes.
2. Add apple juice concentrate and whisk until incorporated.
3. Place the bowl over a pan of simmering water, making sure water does not directly touch the bottom of the bowl. Cook slowly, stirring constantly, until mixture is thick enough to coat the back of a spoon. Do not let the mixture boil. If the mixture gets hotter than 185°F, it will curdle.
4. Immediately remove bowl from heat. With a fine-mesh sieve, strain into a clean bowl. Add applejack; stir until blended.
5. Cool to room temperature, cover sabayon, and refrigerate until ready to finish.
6. In a large bowl and with an electric mixer set on medium speed, whip cream until peaks just begin to hold their shape. Gently fold whipped cream into sabayon.
7. Serve immediately or chilled. If used after an hour, rewhip slightly.

YIELD: *4 cups*

NOTE

❑ *Use half the chilled sabayon base and ¾ cup cream to make 2 cups of finished sauce. The chilled base will keep in the refrigerator for up to 5 days and can be used as a sauce for other desserts.*

RUM RAISIN
❦ BREAD PUDDING

Crunchy coconut fringe crowns a traditional rum raisin custard. To receive raves, prepare this pudding anytime for anyone.

Day-old French bread, cut into ½-inch cubes to equal 6 cups, 20 to 22 ½-inch-thick slices, about 7 to 8 ounces

1	**cup raisins**
¼	**cup dark rum**
5	**large eggs**
1	**cup granulated sugar**
2	**tablespoons vanilla extract**
2	**cups milk**
1	**cup heavy or whipping cream**
1	**cup sweetened, shredded coconut**
2	**tablespoons unsalted butter, melted and cooled slightly**

NOTE

❏ *If you do not have day-old bread, place fresh bread in a 300°F oven until it begins to lose some of its moisture, or leave fresh bread uncovered to air-dry for several hours or overnight.*

1. Generously butter a 2-quart shallow baking dish.

2. Soak raisins in rum for at least 30 minutes.

3. In a large bowl and with an electric mixer set on medium speed, beat together eggs, sugar, and vanilla. Reduce mixer speed to low and add milk and cream; continue beating until well mixed.

4. Place bread cubes in a separate large bowl. With a fine-mesh sieve, strain custard mixture over bread. Add raisins and rum and coconut; with a spoon, toss to combine. Let stand for 30 minutes so that the bread absorbs the liquid.

5. Preheat oven to 350°F.

6. Pour pudding mixture into prepared dish, distributing raisins and coconut evenly. Drizzle top with melted butter.

7. Bake for 45 to 50 minutes, or until custard is set (knife inserted 1 inch from center comes out clean), pudding is puffed, and top is golden brown.

8. Remove from oven onto a wire rack and cool for at least 10 minutes.

9. Spoon onto serving plates. Serve warm, at room temperature, or chilled.

Let unused portions come to room temperature, cover, and refrigerate.

YIELD: *8 servings*

SWEET
BREAD PUDDINGS
MADE FROM
BREADS OTHER
THAN FRENCH
OR ITALIAN

No matter how many bread puddings there are, there is always room for a better and more delicious one. They epitomize hominess and are the embodiment of what we now love—old-fashioned desserts. They should remain what they are meant to be—peasant in character and delicious, not a peasant in emperor's clothes.

My particular favorites are somewhat custardy and made with bread that stands on its own, egg-based bread such as challah or semolina-based bread such as peasant bread. I happen to prefer bread pudding with a side sauce—either a custard sauce, hard sauce, or fruit sauce."

—*Perla Meyers*
Author, Perla Meyers' Art of Seasonal Cooking

CINNAMON BREAD CUSTARD
❦ WITH FRESH BERRIES

Prepared by Bradley Ogden, Chef-Proprietor, Lark Creek Inn, Larkspur, California

Cinnamon-raisin bread, 16 slices

8	tablespoons unsalted butter, melted
4	large eggs
2	large egg yolks
¾	cup granulated sugar
3	cups milk
1	cup heavy or whipping cream
1	tablespoon vanilla extract
	Confectioners' sugar, enough to dust finished pudding
1	cup blueberries
1	cup raspberries
1	cup strawberries, sliced

NOTE

❑ *Packaged, sliced cinnamon-raisin bread works just fine in this recipe, but a bakery-fresh loaf, cut into 8 1-inch-thick slices, will make the dish even better.*

1. Lightly butter a 9- by 12-inch baking dish. Preheat oven to 350°F.

2. Brush both sides of bread slices with melted butter and arrange in rows in prepared dish.

3. In a large bowl, beat together eggs and egg yolks. Whisk in sugar, milk, cream, and vanilla. With a fine-mesh sieve, strain custard mixture over bread slices, making sure that each piece is evenly moistened.

4. Set baking dish in a larger ovenproof pan. Add enough hot water to the pan to come halfway up sides of baking dish.

5. Bake in upper third of oven for 25 to 35 minutes, or until custard is set (knife inserted 1 inch from center comes out clean) and top is lightly browned.

6. Remove from water bath onto a wire rack and let rest for about 15 minutes.

7. Cut into squares, sprinkle lightly with confectioners' sugar, and serve with the berries.

Let unused portions come to room temperature, cover, and refrigerate.

YIELD: *8 servings*

BREAD AND BUTTER PUDDING CAKE
❦ WITH CARAMEL SAUCE

Prepared by John Terczak, Chef-Proprietor, Tamales restaurants in Chicago and Highland Park, Illinois

Firm-textured white sandwich bread, 10 slices

6	tablespoons unsalted butter, softened
2	tablespoons granulated sugar
¼	teaspoon ground cinnamon
1	vanilla bean, split
3	cups milk
3	large eggs
2	large egg yolks
1	cup granulated sugar

Confectioners' sugar, enough to dust serving plates
Caramel Sauce (recipe follows)

NOTE

❑ *When assembling pudding, lean the first circle of toast triangles, points down, against the side of prepared dish. Continue making concentric circles around the dish, pressing against toast pieces to keep them in position, until all triangles are in place and the center is empty. Be confident; this does work.*

1. Generously butter a 1½-quart soufflé or deep-sided baking dish.

2. Butter one side of each bread slice and place on a cookie sheet. Lightly toast, butter side up, under broiler. Lean toast slices against vertical surface to cool so that they won't become soggy.

3. When cool, trim and discard crusts. Cut each slice into 2 triangles. In the prepared dish, make concentric circles of toast triangles with long side of each pointing up (points down). Leave center empty.

4. Combine the 2 tablespoons sugar with cinnamon. Sprinkle over toast and set aside.

5. Preheat oven to 400°F.

6. Scrape soft interior of the split vanilla bean. In a medium saucepan, bring milk almost to a boil with vanilla bean scrapings and bean itself.

7. In a large bowl, beat eggs and egg yolks with the 1 cup sugar until sugar dissolves and mixture is smooth and lemon colored.

8. Gradually add milk, beating continually. Remove froth with a ladle. Remove vanilla bean.

9. Carefully pour custard mixture into the hole in center of toast circles. Do not saturate all bread points with custard mixture.

10. Set prepared dish in a larger ovenproof pan. Add enough hot water to the pan to come halfway up sides of baking dish.

11. Bake for 40 to 50 minutes, or until custard is set and pudding is slightly risen.

12. Remove pudding from water bath onto a wire rack. Cool to room temperature.

13. Dust serving plates with confectioners' sugar. Using a cake knife and rubber scraper, transfer pudding-cake to plates without losing custard. Drizzle Caramel Sauce (recipe follows) around cake and serve at once.

Let unused portions come to room temperature, cover, and refrigerate.

YIELD: *8 servings*

Caramel Sauce

Prepared by John Terczak

1   **tablespoon unsalted butter**
⅓   **cup granulated sugar**
½   **cup heavy or whipping cream**

1. Place butter in a small heavy saucepan. Pour sugar on top of butter; do not stir.

2. Melt sugar and butter over medium heat until mixture is brown and bubbling, about 10 minutes.

3. Whisk and continue cooking caramel until it is very brown and almost to the point of scorching. Immediately begin whisking in small amounts of cream. Continue until caramel has a syrup consistency.

4. Pour caramel sauce through a fine-mesh strainer into top of a double boiler. Keep warm or reheat over hot, but not boiling, water.

This sauce keeps well in the refrigerator for up to 10 days and can be reheated.

YIELD: *Scant 1 cup*

CAPRIOTADA
❧ (MEXICAN BREAD PUDDING)

Prepared by Dawn Bailey, Pastry Chef, John Ash & Co., Santa Rosa, California
Inspired by Diana Kennedy

"People think of bread puddings as homey, old-fashioned desserts and that's why they like them. Restaurants are now putting them on their menus. I've been doing this type of dessert for a long time. I try to keep it simple, but with an elegant twist. It has to catch your eye, but it also has to taste wonderful."

Egg bread, 8 ounces, cut into ½-inch-thick slices

2½   **cups half-and-half**
⅓   **cup granulated sugar**
1   **2-inch piece of cinnamon stick**
⅓   **cup mixed golden raisins and currants**
⅓   **cup blanched, sliced almonds**
6   **tablespoons vegetable oil**
3   **6-inch tortillas**
4   **tablespoons unsalted butter**
½   **cup chopped, candied pineapple**

T O P P I N G

4   **large eggs, separated**
  Pinch of salt
2   **tablespoons granulated sugar**
  Caramel Sauce (page 41)

1. Lightly butter an 8-inch soufflé dish.

2. In a saucepan, place half-and-half, the ⅓ cup sugar, cinnamon, raisins, and almonds. Bring to a simmer; simmer and stir until sugar is dissolved. Remove from heat and cool. When cool, remove cinnamon stick.

3. Heat 2 tablespoons of the oil in a skillet. Fry tortillas on both sides until leathery. Drain and cut into 2-inch pieces and completely cover bottom of prepared dish.

4. Melt together the remaining oil and butter and, with a pastry brush, lightly paint both sides of bread slices. Lightly sauté bread over moderate heat until golden brown.

5. Layer a third of bread slices in the soufflé dish, completely covering tortilla strips. Pour over one fourth of half-and-half mixture; sprinkle on one third of pineapple. Continue layering, ending with half-and-half mixture.

6. Preheat oven to 350°F.

7. In a clean, dry, large bowl, beat egg whites until fluffy. Add salt and beat until stiff. Add egg yolks, one at a time, beating until well combined. Spread topping evenly over pudding and sprinkle with the 2 tablespoons sugar.

8. Bake on lowest shelf of oven for 30 to 35 minutes, until top is golden brown. Remove from oven onto a wire rack.

9. Cut into wedges. Serve hot or at room temperature with warm Caramel Sauce (page 41).

Let unused portions come to room temperature, cover, and refrigerate.

YIELD: *6 servings*

CARAMELIZED APPLE BREAD PUDDING
🍎 WITH CRANBERRIES

Prepared by Wolfgang Puck, Chef-Proprietor, Spago, West Hollywood, California

Cinnamon bread, 1-pound loaf

12 tablespoons unsalted butter, melted
Cinnamon sugar, enough to sprinkle on toast slices

C U S T A R D

1½ cups milk
1½ cups heavy or whipping cream
½ whole nutmeg, grated, or 1½ teaspoons gound nutmeg
1 vanilla bean, split and scraped
2 cinnamon sticks
2 large egg yolks
2 large eggs
¼ cup firmly packed brown sugar

C A R A M E L I Z E D   A P P L E S

12 tablespoons unsalted butter
1 vanilla bean, split and scraped
6 Granny Smith apples, peeled, cored, and thinly sliced
½ cup firmly packed brown sugar
1 cup fresh cranberries
2 tablespoons bourbon

C A R A M E L

⅓ cup granulated sugar
3 tablespoons water
Confectioners' sugar, enough to dust finished pudding

NOTE

❑ *We love caramel and made more than called for in this recipe. We used 2 cups granulated sugar and 1 cup water. We increased the baking time to 1 hour and 30 minutes.*

1. Brush a 9- by 13- by 2-inch cake pan with butter.

2. Toast slices of cinnamon bread. Brush them with the 12 tablespoons melted butter and sprinkle with cinnamon sugar. Set aside.

3. Prepare custard. In a small heavy saucepan, bring milk, cream, nutmeg, vanilla bean, and cinnamon sticks to a boil. Remove from heat and let steep, covered, for 30 minutes. Cream together egg yolks, eggs, and the ¼ cup brown sugar. Pour milk mixture over eggs, whisk together, strain, and set aside.

44

4. Prepare apples. In a heavy-bottom sauté pan, heat the 12 tablespoons butter and vanilla bean until butter almost browns. Add apples and the ½ cup brown sugar. Sauté apples until lightly caramelized and tender. Add cranberries and cook for another 5 minutes. Add bourbon. Remove from heat and allow to cool. Remove vanilla bean and discard.

5. Prepare caramel. In a small heavy saucepan over medium heat, caramelize the granulated sugar and water. Coat bottom of prepared cake pan evenly with caramel.

6. Preheat oven to 350°F.

7. Soak cinnamon toast in custard until soft.

8. Layer bottom of pan with a third of the soaked bread slices. Top with a third of the caramelized apples. Pour a third of the custard onto the apples. Repeat with bread, apples, and custard two more times so that the apples and custard are on top of dish.

9. Cover pan with aluminum foil. Set pan in a larger ovenproof pan. Add enough hot water to come halfway up sides of smaller pan.

10. Bake for 1 hour, or until custard is set (knife inserted 1 inch from center comes out clean).

11. Remove from water bath onto a wire rack and cool for 30 minutes. Sprinkle confectioners' sugar on top.

12. Cut into serving pieces. Serve with freshly whipped cream flavored with a touch of bourbon.

Let unused portions come to room temperature, cover, and refrigerate.

YIELD: *10 servings*

MOSTLY MERINGUE
❦ BREAD PUDDING PUFFS

Surprise—make a bread pudding in disguise! These chewy, individual meringue puffs, filled with toasted pecans and chopped dates, improve with age.

Firm-textured white bread, processed into medium-fine crumbs to equal 1½ cups, toasted in a 300°F oven for 10 to 15 minutes, cooled to room temperature, approximately 4 slices

3	large egg whites, ⅓ cup
1	teaspoon baking powder
1	cup granulated sugar
1	teaspoon vanilla extract
½	cup chopped pecans, toasted in a 350°F oven for 7 to 10 minutes
½	cup chopped dates

1. Set aside two parchment-lined cookie sheets. Preheat oven to 300°F.

2. In a clean, dry, large bowl and with an electric mixer set on medium-low speed, beat egg whites until foamy. Increase mixer speed to medium-high, beating continuously until they form soft peaks. Gradually add baking powder, sugar, and vanilla; beat until stiff and glossy.

3. Gently fold bread crumbs, pecans, and dates into meringue.

4. Drop meringue by large tablespoons, one inch apart, onto prepared cookie sheets.

5. Bake for 15 minutes, or until meringues are pale tan.

6. Remove from oven onto a wire rack. Cool for 10 minutes and remove meringues from parchment paper. Let stand several hours.

7. Serve at room temperature with Spa Chocolate Sauce (page 13), 1 tablespoon sauce for each meringue, or sweetened whipped cream, or both.

Unused portions should be stored in an airtight container.

YIELD: *20 to 22 individual meringues*

TANGY LEMON
❦ BREAD PUDDING SOUFFLÉ

Served warm, this pudding resembles a soufflé. Served cold, you could be eating lemon bars. This refreshing pudding has just the right amount of tartness, a lovely dessert for any meal.

Day-old, firm-textured white bread, crusts removed, cut into ½-inch cubes to equal 3 generous cups, approximately 6 slices

5	teaspoons grated lemon zest, 2 to 3 lemons
1	cup heavy or whipping cream
1	cup milk
1	cup granulated sugar
3	tablespoons unsalted butter, cut into small pieces
½	teaspoon salt
4	large eggs, separated
½	cup fresh lemon juice
	Pinch of salt
	Confectioners' sugar, enough to dust finished pudding

NOTES

❏ *If you do not have day-old bread, place fresh bread in a 300°F oven until it begins to lose some of its moisture, or leave fresh bread uncovered to air-dry for several hours or overnight.*
❏ *Expect the bread soufflé to fall as it cools.*

1. Generously butter the bottom of a 2-quart shallow baking dish. Preheat oven to 325°F.

2. In a large bowl, combine bread cubes and zest.

3. In a small heavy saucepan, combine cream, milk, sugar, butter, and the ½ teaspoon salt. Over medium heat, cook until butter melts, stirring occasionally. Remove from heat and pour over bread and zest; with a spoon, toss to combine. Cool slightly.

4. In a small bowl, whisk together egg yolks and lemon juice. Add to bread mixture and stir gently. Set aside.

5. In a clean, dry, large bowl and with an electric mixer set on medium-low speed, beat egg whites and the pinch of salt until foamy. Increase mixer speed to medium-high, beating continuously until stiff but not dry. Gently fold whites into pudding mixture.

6. Pour pudding mixture into prepared dish.

7. Bake for 50 to 60 minutes, or until the custard is set (knife inserted 1 inch from center comes out clean) and top is golden brown.

8. Remove from oven onto a wire rack and cool for 10 minutes. Dust pudding with confectioners' sugar.

9. Spoon onto serving plates. Serve warm, at room temperature, or chilled with a simple raspberry sauce.

Let unused portions come to room temperature, cover, and refrigerate.

YIELD: *8 servings*

PHYLLIS'S SOUR CHERRY
❧ BREAKFAST BREAD PUDDING

This is a very special cinnamon French toast breakfast dish studded with rum-soaked cherries. Attractive to serve, delicious to taste, it starts the day with flair.

Good-quality bakery cinnamon bread, 12 slices, cut into halves on the diagonal, about 1 pound

¾   **cup dried cherries, chopped**
¼   **cup dark rum**
5½ **cups milk**
6   **large eggs**
1   **large egg yolk**
1   **cup granulated sugar**
1   **tablespoon vanilla extract**
½   **teaspoon ground cinnamon**
3   **tablespoons granulated sugar**
¾   **cup chopped pecans, toasted in a 350°F oven for 7 to 10 minutes**
1   **tablespoon butter, cut into small pieces**
    Confectioners' sugar, enough to dust finished pudding

1. Generously butter a 2½-quart shallow baking dish.

2. Soak cherries in rum for at least 30 minutes. Drain and discard rum.

3. Arrange bread diagonals in prepared dish in an overlapping pattern, fallen-domino fashion. Top with cherries. Set aside.

4. In a medium-size heavy saucepan over medium heat, bring milk almost to a boil.

5. In a large bowl and with an electric mixer set on medium speed, beat together eggs, egg yolk, the 1 cup sugar, and vanilla. Gradually add milk, beating continually until incorporated. Skim and discard foam.

6. Carefully pour custard mixture over bread. Cover with plastic wrap and press down with your hands or back of a spoon so that the bread absorbs the liquid. Let stand for 30 minutes.

7. Preheat oven to 300°F.

8. In a small bowl, combine cinnamon and the 3 tablespoons sugar.

9. Remove plastic wrap from pudding. Sprinkle top with cinnamon-sugar and pecans. Dot with butter.

10. Set baking dish in a larger ovenproof pan. Add enough hot water to the pan to come halfway up sides of baking dish.

11. Bake for 1 hour and 10 minutes, or until custard is set (knife inserted 1 inch from center comes out clean).

12. Remove from water bath onto a rack and cool for at least 20 minutes.

13. Preheat broiler. Dust pudding with confectioners' sugar and broil about 6 inches from heat until top is glazed. Be careful not to burn. Remove from oven.

14. Spoon onto serving plates. Serve warm with maple syrup.

Let unused portions come to room temperature, cover, and refrigerate.

YIELD: *10 servings*

PRUNE AND PORT
❦ PUDDING

This is comfort food on a grand scale—a must for prune Danish lovers. Linda finds this irresistible, a dish with grace and charm.

Day-old, firm-textured white bread, 10 slices

1½	**cups coarsely chopped, dried, pitted prunes**
⅓	**cup raisins**
¼	**cup ruby port**
6	**tablespoons unsalted butter, melted**
2	**cups heavy or whipping cream**
1¾	**cups milk**
5	**large eggs**
4	**large egg yolks**
½	**cup granulated sugar**
1	**tablespoon vanilla extract**
	Pinch of salt
3	**tablespoons granulated sugar**

NOTES

❑ *If you do not have day-old bread, place fresh bread in a 300°F oven until it begins to lose some of its moisture, or leave fresh bread uncovered to air-dry for several hours or overnight.*
❑ *Additional prunes may be soaked in port, puréed, and incorporated into sweetened whipped cream.*
❑ *A better brand of port enhances the taste of this pudding.*

1. Generously butter a 2½-quart soufflé or deep-sided baking dish.

2. Soak prunes and raisins in port for at least 30 minutes.

3. Brush one side of each bread slice with melted butter and cut into quarters.

4. Arrange a third of the bread quarters, buttered side up, in prepared dish in an overlapping pattern. Spoon half of the fruit and port over bread. Repeat layering, ending with bread quarters.

5. In a small heavy saucepan over medium heat, bring cream and milk almost to a boil.

6. In a large bowl and with an electric mixer set on medium speed, beat together eggs, egg yolks, and the ½ cup sugar, vanilla, and salt. Gradually add cream mixture, beating continually until incorporated. Skim and discard foam.

7. Carefully pour custard mixture over bread. Cover with plastic wrap and press down with your hands or back of a spoon so that the bread absorbs the liquid. Let stand for 30 minutes.

8. Preheat oven to 325°F.

9. Remove plastic wrap from pudding. Sprinkle top with the 3 tablespoons sugar.

10. Set baking dish in a larger ovenproof pan. Add enough hot water to the pan to come halfway up sides of baking dish.

11. Bake for 1 hour and 10 minutes, or until custard is set (knife inserted 1 inch from center comes out clean) and top is golden brown.

12. Remove from water bath onto a wire rack and cool for at least 10 minutes.

13. Spoon onto serving plates. Serve warm or at room temperature with sweetened whipped cream.

Let unused portions come to room temperature, cover, and refrigerate.

YIELD: *10 servings*

RAISIN–RAISIN BREAD PUDDING
❦ WITH VANILLA CUSTARD SAUCE

An old-fashioned bread pudding prepared in an old-fashioned way, this dense dessert is filled with raisins and spice and a touch of Madeira. Serve with a puddle of pure Vanilla Custard.

Day-old, firm-textured white bread, 1-pound loaf, crusts removed, torn into pieces to equal 8 generous cups, approximately 16 slices

4   cups milk
8   tablespoons unsalted butter, cut into small pieces
3⅓   cups raisins, equal amounts of dark and golden
    Grated zest of 1 orange
1   tablespoon all-purpose flour
½   teaspoon salt
1   teaspoon ground cloves
1   teaspoon ground cinnamon
1   teaspoon grated nutmeg
5   large eggs
1   cup granulated sugar
⅓   cup Madeira
1   teaspoon vanilla extract
    Vanilla Custard Sauce (recipe follows)

1. Generously butter a 2½-quart shallow baking dish. Preheat oven to 300°F.

2. In a medium-size heavy saucepan over medium heat, bring milk almost to a boil.

3. Place bread pieces and butter in a very large bowl. Pour milk over bread and butter and stir. Add raisins, zest, flour, salt, cloves, cinnamon, and nutmeg to bread mixture; stir until incorporated.

4. In a large bowl, whisk together eggs, sugar, Madeira, and vanilla. Add to bread mixture and stir until well mixed.

5. Pour pudding mixture into prepared dish, distributing raisins evenly.

6. Bake for 1 hour and 30 minutes, or until custard is set (knife inserted 1 inch from center comes out clean) and top is browned.

7. Remove from oven onto a wire rack and cool for at least 10 minutes.

8. Spoon onto serving plates. Serve warm with plenty of Vanilla

Custard Sauce (recipe follows), 2 to 3 tablespoons sauce for each, or Brandy Hard Sauce (page 27), 2 tablespoons sauce for each serving.

Let unused portions come to room temperature, cover, and refrigerate.

YIELD: *10 servings*

Vanilla Custard Sauce

6   **large egg yolks**
⅔   **cup granulated sugar**
2   **cups half-and-half**
2   **teaspoons vanilla extract**

NOTE

❑ *This recipe may be halved.*

1. In a medium-size stainless-steel bowl, whisk egg yolks and sugar until sugar dissolves and mixture is lemon colored, 5 minutes.

2. In a small heavy saucepan over medium heat, bring half-and-half almost to a boil.

3. Gradually add half-and-half to egg mixture, whisking continually until incorporated.

4. Place the bowl over a pan of simmering water, making sure water does not directly touch the bottom of the bowl. Cook slowly, stirring constantly, until mixture is thick enough to coat the back of a spoon. Do not let the mixture boil. If the mixture gets hotter than 185°F, it will curdle.

5. Immediately remove bowl from heat and, with a fine-mesh sieve, strain into a clean bowl. Add vanilla; stir until blended. Continue to stir to help cooling process, 1 to 2 minutes.

6. Cool to room temperature, cover, and refrigerate until ready to use. Serve chilled.

YIELD: *2½ cups*

SHERRIED BREAD PUDDING
❦ WITH CITRON AND CURRANTS

This is where it all began: the authors' sentimental favorite, their first taste of bread pudding. Rich egg bread, smooth custard, a hint of sherry, currants, citron, and almonds all combine for a new classic. Linda and Barbara have served this for dessert and breakfast, for family and friends—with great reviews.

Day-old challah or other egg bread, crusts removed, cut into ½-inch cubes to equal 4 cups, about 5 ounces with crusts

NOTE

❑ *If you do not have day-old bread, place fresh bread in a 300°F oven until it begins to lose some of its moisture, or leave fresh bread uncovered to air-dry for several hours or overnight.*

3   **tablespoons currants**
¼   **cup dry sherry**
4   **large eggs**
½   **cup superfine sugar**
1   **teaspoon vanilla extract**
¼   **teaspoon salt**
¼   **teaspoon grated nutmeg**
1¼   **cups heavy or whipping cream**
½   **cup milk**
    Grated zest of 1 orange
⅓   **cup plus 2 tablespoons candied citron, finely chopped**
⅓   **cup slivered almonds**
    Confectioners' sugar, enough to dust finished pudding

1. Lightly butter a 9-inch deep-sided ceramic pie dish.

2. Soak currants in sherry for at least 30 minutes.

3. In a large bowl and with an electric mixer set on medium speed, beat together eggs, sugar, vanilla, salt, and nutmeg. Reduce mixer speed to low and add cream and milk; continue beating until well mixed.

4. Place bread cubes in a separate large bowl. With a fine-mesh sieve, strain custard mixture over bread. Add currants and sherry, zest, and citron; with a spoon, toss to combine. Let stand for 30 minutes so that the bread absorbs the liquid.

5. Preheat oven to 350°F.

6. Pour pudding mixture into prepared dish, distributing currants evenly. Sprinkle top with almonds.

7. Bake for 50 to 55 minutes, or until custard is set (knife inserted 1 inch from center comes out clean), pudding is puffed, and top is golden brown.

8. Remove from oven onto a wire rack and cool for at least 20 minutes. Dust pudding generously with confectioners' sugar.

9. Cut into wedges. Serve warm, at room temperature, or chilled.

Let unused portions come to room temperature, cover, and refrigerate.

YIELD: *6 servings*

STREUSEL COFFEE CAKE
❦ BREAD PUDDING

Bread pudding takes a crunchy turn. This is a very moist breakfast cake, perfect with a cup of coffee and a group of friends and neighbors.

Firm-textured white bread, 1-pound loaf, processed into coarse crumbs to equal 8 cups, approximately 16 slices

2½	cups milk
2½	cups heavy or whipping cream
6	large eggs
1½	cups granulated sugar
2	teaspoons vanilla extract
½	teaspoon ground cinnamon
¼	teaspoon grated nutmeg
	Grated zest of 1 lemon

S T R E U S E L

½	cup firmly packed light brown sugar
2	tablespoons all-purpose flour
½	teaspoon ground cinnamon
3	tablespoons unsalted butter, melted
1⅓	cups chopped walnuts, toasted in a 350°F oven for 7 to 10 minutes

S Y R U P

½	cup granulated sugar
½	teaspoon ground cinnamon
¼	cup water

1. Generously butter a 9- by 13- by 2-inch baking pan.

2. Place bread crumbs in a very large bowl. Add milk and cream and stir. Let stand for 15 minutes so that the bread absorbs the liquid.

3. Preheat oven to 400°F.

4. In a large bowl and with an electric mixer set on medium speed, beat together eggs, the 1½ cups granulated sugar, vanilla, ½ teaspoon cinnamon, nutmeg, and zest. Add to bread mixture and stir until well mixed. Set batter aside.

5. Prepare streusel. In a small bowl, combine brown sugar, flour, ½ teaspoon cinnamon, melted butter, and walnuts. Set aside.

6. Prepare syrup. In a small heavy saucepan over medium heat, combine the ½ cup granulated sugar, ½ teaspoon cinnamon, and water. Cook until sugar dissolves, 3 minutes. Remove from heat.

7. Pour half of the batter into prepared pan. Top with half of the streusel; with a knife, swirl streusel into batter. Add the remaining batter. Pour the syrup over pudding mixture in a zigzag pattern.

8. Bake for 20 minutes. Top with the remaining streusel. Bake for an additional 25 to 30 minutes, or until pudding is puffed and top is browned.

9. Remove from oven onto a wire rack and cool for 20 minutes.

10. Cut into squares. Serve warm or at room temperature.

Let unused portions come to room temperature, cover, and refrigerate.

YIELD: *12 servings*

WINTER SPICED GERMAN STEAMED
❧ BREAD PUDDING

This is a good-natured pudding. It does take time, but it is very simple to make. Raisins and walnuts are steamed with winter spices for a cold-weather favorite, ideal for a day at home.

Day-old, firm-textured white bread, torn into pieces to equal 2 cups, 3 to 4 slices

⅔	**cup granulated sugar**
4	**tablespoons unsalted butter, cut into small pieces**
1	**cup raisins**
½	**cup chopped walnuts**
¾	**teaspoon ground cinnamon**
¼	**teaspoon grated nutmeg**
¼	**teaspoon ground cloves**
1	**teaspoon baking soda**
1	**cup boiling water**
	Heavy or whipping cream, enough to sauce finished pudding

NOTES

❑ *If you do not have day-old bread, place fresh bread in a 300°F oven until it begins to lose some of its moisture, or leave fresh bread uncovered to air-dry for several hours or overnight.*
❑ *The pudding in the top of the double boiler doesn't need a babysitter, so don't peek.*
❑ *A glass double boiler is helpful in regulating the simmer.*
❑ *Golden raisins may be used.*

1. In the top of a 1½-quart double boiler, place bread cubes, sugar, butter, raisins, walnuts, cinnamon, nutmeg, and cloves.

2. In a medium bowl, dissolve baking soda in boiling water.

3. Pour water over bread mixture and gently stir until bread is moistened and ingredients are evenly distributed.

4. Cover top of double boiler and, over gently simmering water, steam pudding for 3 hours, making sure water comes halfway up sides of top. The pudding must stay covered for entire cooking time.

5. Remove from heat, uncover, and cool slightly.

6. Spoon into serving bowls. Serve warm or at room temperature with 1 to 2 tablespoons heavy cream.

Let unused portions come to room temperature, cover, and refrigerate.

YIELD: *6 servings*

SWEET BREAD PUDDINGS MADE FROM NOVELTY BREADS

Bread pudding—the very name promises so much. Yet the taste, the texture, are so easy to achieve. It's a family favorite."

—*Bernard Clayton, Jr.*
Author, Bernard Clayton's Cooking Across America

COCONUT
❦ RUM CUSTARD

Discover this multilayered treasure of caramel, delicate ladyfingers, rum custard, and coconut meringue.

Small ladyfingers, equal to 3 ounces, approximately 24

¼   **cup currants**
⅓   **cup dark rum**
¾   **cup granulated sugar**
3   **tablespoons water**
⅛   **teaspoon cream of tartar**
1   **14-ounce can sweetened condensed milk**
½   **cup canned cream of coconut**
¾   **cup water**
3   **large eggs**
2   **large egg yolks**
1   **teaspoon vanilla extract**

T O P P I N G

2   **large egg whites**
⅛   **teaspoon cream of tartar**
4   **tablespoons granulated sugar**
2   **tablespoons sweetened, shredded coconut**

1. Lightly butter a 7- by 11-inch baking pan.

2. Soak currants in rum for at least 30 minutes.

3. In a small heavy saucepan, combine the ¾ cup sugar, the 3 tablespoons water, and ⅛ teaspoon cream of tartar. Over medium-low heat, swirl until sugar dissolves. Increase heat to medium-high and continue cooking, without stirring, until syrup is a deep golden brown, 12 to 15 minutes. Immediately pour syrup into prepared pan, turning rapidly to coat bottom.

4. Arrange ladyfingers in bottom of pan; sprinkle with currants and rum.

5. Preheat oven to 325°F.

6. In a large bowl, whisk sweetened condensed milk, cream of coconut, the ¾ cup water, eggs, egg yolks, and vanilla until smooth. With a fine-mesh sieve, strain custard mixture over ladyfingers.

7. Set baking pan in a larger ovenproof pan. Add enough hot water to the pan to come halfway up sides of smaller pan.

8. Bake for 50 minutes, or until top is firm to the touch and lightly browned.

9. Remove from water bath onto a wire rack and cool to room temperature. (At this point, pudding can be refrigerated several hours or overnight.)

10. Prepare topping. In a clean, dry, large bowl and with an electric mixer set on medium-low speed, beat egg whites and ⅛ teaspoon cream of tartar until foamy. Increase mixer speed to medium-high and gradually add the 4 tablespoons sugar, beating continuously until stiff but not dry.

11. Preheat broiler. Top pudding with meringue, spreading to the edges. Sprinkle with coconut. Broil about 6 inches from heat until lightly golden, 30 to 60 seconds.

12. Remove from oven onto a wire rack, cool to room temperature, and refrigerate.

13. Cut into squares. Serve chilled, sauced with its own caramel syrup.

YIELD: *8 servings*

GINGERBREAD PUDDING
❦ WITH WARM VANILLA BUTTER SAUCE

A moist gingerbread dessert—a pudding, a cake, and a brownie—combines cinnamon and cloves with raisins and pecans and reminds us of our childhood. Serve with smooth and rich Warm Vanilla Butter Sauce to complete the memory.

Granny's Gingerbread (recipe follows), lightly packed crumbs to equal 2 cups

5	tablespoons unsalted butter, softened
½	cup granulated sugar
1	large egg
½	cup dark molasses
½	teaspoon baking soda
½	cup buttermilk
¼	cup all-purpose flour
¼	teaspoon salt
1	teaspoon ground cinnamon
½	teaspoon ground cloves
½	cup raisins
½	cup chopped pecans
	Warm Vanilla Butter Sauce (recipe follows)

1. Generously butter an 8-inch square baking pan. Preheat oven to 350°F.

2. In a large bowl and with an electric mixer set on medium speed, cream butter, sugar, and egg until light and fluffy. Reduce mixer speed to low and add molasses, beating until thoroughly blended. Scrape down sides of bowl as necessary.

3. Mix baking soda into buttermilk and gradually add to creamed mixture.

4. Sift together flour, salt, cinnamon, and cloves. Beat into butter mixture until incorporated.

5. Add gingerbread crumbs, raisins, and pecans. Stir until well mixed.

6. Pour pudding mixture into prepared pan. Cover with aluminum foil.

7. Bake for 30 minutes. Uncover and bake for an additional 10 to 15 minutes, or until pudding is set (toothpick inserted comes out clean) and begins to pull away from sides of pan. Do not overbake.

8. Remove from oven onto a wire rack and cool for at least 15 minutes.

9. Cut into squares. Serve warm or at room temperature with Warm Vanilla Butter Sauce (recipe follows), 2 generous tablespoons sauce for each serving, or Mary's Apple Sabayon (page 35), ¼ cup sauce for each serving.

Let unused portions come to room temperature, cover, and refrigerate.

YIELD: *9 servings*

Granny's Gingerbread

NOTE

❑ *One third of this recipe is needed for Gingerbread Pudding.*

¼ **cup vegetable oil**
¼ **cup granulated sugar**
¼ **cup dark molasses**
1 **cup all-purpose flour**
½ **teaspoon baking soda**
¼ **teaspoon salt**
½ **teaspoon ground ginger**
½ **teaspoon ground cinnamon**
½ **cup hot water**

1. Generously butter an 8-inch baking pan. Preheat oven to 350°F.

2. In a large bowl and with an electric mixer set on low speed, beat oil, sugar, and molasses until combined.

3. Sift together flour, baking soda, salt, ginger, and cinnamon and add to oil mixture alternately with the hot water, beating after each addition until smooth.

4. Pour batter into prepared pan.

5. Bake for 20 minutes, or until cake pulls away from sides of pan.

6. Remove from oven onto a wire rack and cool for at least 10 minutes.

7. Cut into squares. Reserve 2 cups of crumbs for pudding. The remainder may be served warm or at room temperature with Warm Vanilla Butter Sauce (recipe follows) or Mary's Apple Sabayon (page 35).

Let unused portions come to room temperature, cover, and refrigerate.

YIELD: *9 servings*

Warm Vanilla Butter Sauce

1   **cup granulated sugar**
½   **cup heavy or whipping cream**
8   **tablespoons butter**
1   **teaspoon vanilla extract**

1. In a small heavy saucepan, combine sugar, cream, and butter. Over medium heat, cook, stirring occasionally, until butter is melted and sugar is dissolved.
2. Remove from heat and add vanilla.
3. Serve warm.

This sauce keeps well in the refrigerator for up to 10 days and can be reheated.

YIELD: *1½ cups*

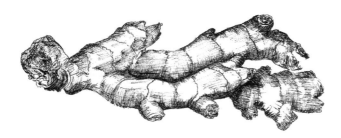

KAHLÚA
❦ BREAD PUDDING

Remember bread in a can? It's back! Fine crumbs of New England brown bread, soaked in coffee-flavored custard, result in a rich, dense, tortelike dessert.

New England brown bread, with or without raisins, 1-pound can, processed into fine crumbs to equal 4 cups

NOTE

❑ *Serve with any of the caramel sauces in this book. Use 2 tablespoons sauce for each serving.*

1¾ **cups milk**
4   **tablespoons unsalted butter, cut into tablespoons**
¼   **cup firmly packed dark brown sugar**
½   **cup chopped dates**
¼   **teaspoon salt**
3   **large eggs**
⅓   **cup Kahlúa or other coffee-flavored liqueur**
    Confectioners' sugar, enough to dust finished pudding

1. Generously butter a 9½-inch springform pan. Cover outside of springform pan with foil to prevent leakage of pudding from seam.

2. In a small heavy saucepan, combine milk, butter, brown sugar, dates, and salt. Over medium heat, cook until butter melts, stirring occasionally. Cool to lukewarm.

3. In a large bowl and with an electric mixer set on medium speed, beat eggs, milk mixture, and Kahlúa until well mixed.

4. Stir in bread crumbs and let stand for at least 30 minutes so that the bread absorbs the liquid.

5. Preheat oven to 350°F.

6. Pour pudding mixture into prepared pan and bake for 40 to 45 minutes, or until pudding is set (toothpick inserted comes out clean) and top is firm to the touch.

7. Remove from oven onto a wire rack and cool for at least 2 hours.

8. Remove rim of springform pan. Run a sharp knife along the bottom of the pudding and carefully invert onto a plate. Invert again onto a serving platter so that the top of the pudding is facing up. Dust pudding with confectioners' sugar.

9. Cut into wedges. Serve slightly warm or at room temperature with sweetened whipped cream or a caramel sauce.

Let unused portions come to room temperature, cover, and refrigerate.

YIELD: *10 servings*

PEAR CORNMEAL
❧ BREAD PUDDING

Prepared by Emily Luchetti, Pastry Chef at Stars in San Francisco. From *Star Desserts* by Emily Luchetti. Copyright © 1991 by Emily Luchetti. Reprinted by permission of HarperCollins Publishing Inc.

"Pear Cornmeal Bread Pudding is a great warm dessert, and offers more than a custard; it has texture and goodies inside, and instills memories of after-school treats made by Mom."

Cornmeal Poundcake (recipe follows), 5 slices, cut into pieces 1 inch by ½ inch

7	**large eggs**
5	**large egg yolks**
1	**cup granulated sugar**
	Pinch of salt
2½	**cups heavy or whipping cream**
3½	**cups milk**
	One-inch piece of vanilla bean
1½	**pounds pears, peeled, cored, and diced into ½-inch pieces**
	OR
4	**ounces dried pears, cut into ⅜-inch pieces**
½	**teaspoon freshly grated nutmeg, divided**
	Chantilly Cream (recipe follows)

NOTES

❏ *The recipe is an efficient way to use leftover poundcake, brioche, gingerbread, or raisin bread.*
❏ *Numerous variations are possible; try using different fruit fillings (berries, peaches, and pears) as well as different custards (orange, caramel, and ginger). This gives the cook a great deal of creativity.*
❏ *We found the dried pears worked better for us.*

1. Lightly butter a 2½-quart, 3-inch-deep baking dish.

2. In a stainless-steel bowl, whisk together eggs, egg yolks, sugar, and salt. Set mixture aside.

3. In a heavy-bottomed saucepot, bring cream, milk, and vanilla bean almost to a boil. Slowly whisk hot mixture into egg yolks. Cool and, with a fine-mesh sieve, strain custard base.

4. Preheat oven to 325°F.

5. Place pears in bottom of prepared baking dish. Arrange cake pieces on top of pears. Pour custard base over pears. Grate ¼ teaspoon of the nutmeg on top. Set baking dish in a larger ovenproof pan. Add enough hot water to the pan to come halfway up sides of baking dish.

6. Bake pudding, uncovered, for 55 to 60 minutes. A paring knife inserted into custard should come out almost completely clean.

7. Remove from water bath onto a wire rack and cool for at least 10 minutes.

8. To serve the pudding, spoon some into bowls. Top with Chantilly Cream (recipe follows) and the remaining ¼ teaspoon of grated nutmeg.

Let unused portions come to room temperature, cover, and refrigerate.

YIELD: *8 servings*

Cornmeal Poundcake

Prepared by Emily Luchetti

5   tablespoons unsalted butter, softened
1   cup firmly packed brown sugar
½   cup granulated sugar
5   large eggs
¾   cup sour cream
¾   teaspoon almond extract
½   teaspoon vanilla extract
     Pinch of salt
1¼ cups all-purpose flour
1½ teaspoons baking powder
1   cup cornmeal

1. Butter a 9½- by 5½- by 3-inch loaf pan. Preheat oven to 350°F.

2. In a large bowl and with an electric mixer (paddle attachment) set on medium-high speed, combine butter, brown sugar, and granulated sugar and beat for 2 minutes, until light and fluffy.

3. Continuing to mix, add eggs one at a time.

4. Stir in sour cream and almond and vanilla extracts on medium-low speed, mixing well.

5. Sift together salt, flour, and baking powder. On low speed, fold dry ingredients and cornmeal into butter mixture. Pour batter into prepared pan.

6. Bake poundcake for 50 minutes, or until a skewer inserted in middle comes out clean.

7. Remove from oven onto a wire rack. Cool cake.

8. Unmold cake by running a knife around inside edge and inverting the pan.

YIELD: *One 9½- by 5½- by 3-inch loaf*

Chantilly Cream

Prepared by Emily Luchetti

2¼ cups heavy or whipping cream (not ultra-pasteurized)
1   teaspoon vanilla extract
1½ tablespoons granulated sugar
     Small pinch of salt

1. Place all ingredients in a large stainless-steel bowl.
2. Whisk cream until it holds its shape.
3. Refrigerate cream until ready to use. Chantilly Cream should be used within an hour after it is made. If you wait longer to use it, you may need to rewhip it slightly.

YIELD: *4½ cups*

Cornmeal Poundcake and Chantilly Cream are from *Star Desserts* by Emily Luchetti. Copyright © 1991 by Emily Luchetti. Reprinted by permission of HarperCollins Publishers Inc.

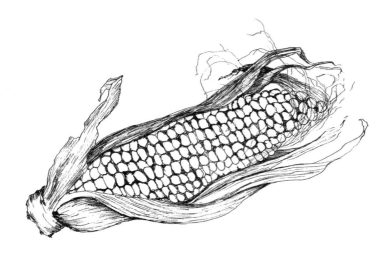

PLUM ALMOND
❦ BREAD PUDDING TART

This dressy dessert pudding combines tart plums, a triple dose of almonds, and flaky croissants. Serve for those very special occasions; reheat leftovers for a memorable breakfast.

Small day-old croissants, about 6 ounces, cut crosswise into ½-inch-thick slices or rounds to equal 4 cups, 6 to 9 croissants

3   **firm plums**
1½   **cups milk**
3   **ounces almond paste, cut into ½-inch pieces, divided**
1   **cup granulated sugar**
4   **large eggs**
1   **teaspoon vanilla extract**
½   **teaspoon almond extract**
⅓   **cup sliced almonds**

NOTE

❑ *Fresh croissants may be used. Place fresh croissant slices in a 300°F oven until lightly toasted, 10 minutes, turning once.*

1. Generously butter a 2-quart ceramic quiche or shallow baking dish.

2. Core plums and quarter; cut quarters in half crosswise.

3. In a small heavy saucepan over medium heat, bring milk almost to a boil.

4. In a large bowl and with an electric mixer set on medium speed, beat half the almond paste, sugar, and 1 egg until nearly smooth. Add the remaining eggs and extracts; beat until blended. Gradually add milk, beating continually until incorporated. Skim and discard foam.

5. Add croissant slices, the remaining almond paste, and plums to custard mixture; with a spoon, toss to combine.

6. Pour pudding mixture into prepared dish. Cover with plastic wrap and press down with your hands or back of a spoon so that the croissants absorb the liquid. Let stand for 1 hour.

7. Preheat oven to 350°F.

8. Remove plastic wrap from pudding. Sprinkle top with almonds.

9. Set baking dish in a larger ovenproof pan. Add enough hot water to the pan to come halfway up sides of baking dish.

10. Bake for 55 minutes, or until custard is set (knife inserted 1 inch from center comes out clean).

11. Remove from water bath onto a wire rack and cool for at least 20 minutes.

12. Cut into wedges. Serve warm or at room temperature with Vanilla Custard Sauce (page 53), 2 to 3 tablespoons sauce for each serving.

Let unused portions come to room temperature, cover, and refrigerate.

YIELD: *10 servings*

SHAPIRO'S DANISH BREAD PUDDING
❦ WITH RUM SAUCE

Prepared by Tom Poulsen, Chef, Shapiro's Delicatessen and Cafeteria, Indianapolis

Day-old Danish (made from a yeast dough), 2 to 2½ pounds (¾ fruit, ¼ cinnamon), chopped into ½-inch chunks to equal 11 to 13 cups

6   extra-large eggs
⅔   cup plus 1 tablespoon granulated sugar
1   cup heavy or whipping cream
1   cup milk
1   tablespoon vanilla extract
1   teaspoon ground cinnamon
1   teaspoon grated nutmeg
2   tablespoons chopped walnuts
     Rum Sauce (recipe follows)

NOTES

❏ *Make a rum sauce using a heavy pastry cream, about 1 cup. Whisk in ¼ cup each of heavy cream and milk. Add a splash of rum and scant teaspoon vanilla.*
❏ *The better quality the Danish, the better tasting the pudding. This recipe was tested with a combination of good-quality cherry, apricot, cheese, and an alligator-cinnamon Danish.*
❏ *Day-old muffins may be substituted for part of the Danish.*
❏ *When adding the cinnamon, nutmeg, and walnuts, barely swirl. Do not overmix.*

1. Lightly butter a 10- by 10- by 2-inch baking pan. Preheat oven to 335°F.

2. Place chunked Danish in prepared pan. Pack lightly.

3. Whisk eggs in a large bowl. Add sugar, cream, milk, and vanilla; continue whisking until well mixed.

4. With a fine-mesh sieve, strain custard mixture over Danish. Sprinkle top with cinnamon, nutmeg, and walnuts. With a knife, swirl through pudding mixture once or twice.

5. Bake for 45 minutes. Cover with aluminum foil and bake for an additional 15 to 20 minutes, or until custard is set (knife inserted 1 inch from center comes out clean) and pudding is firm to the touch.

6. Remove from oven onto a wire rack and cool to room temperature. Cover and refrigerate several hours or overnight.

7. Before serving, remove from refrigerator and bring to room temperature. Cut into squares and serve with Rum Sauce (see Notes or the following recipe), a generous 2 tablespoons sauce for each serving.

Let unused portions come to room temperature, cover, and refrigerate.

YIELD: *12 servings*

Rum Sauce

Adapted from Tom Poulsen

1   cup heavy or whipping cream
⅔   cup Vanilla Custard Sauce (page 53)
1   tablespoon dark rum
1   tablespoon vanilla extract

1. In a large bowl and with an electric mixer set on medium speed, whip cream until peaks just begin to hold their shape.

2. Gently fold Vanilla Custard Sauce, rum, and vanilla into whipped cream.

3. Cover and refrigerate until ready to use. Serve chilled. Sauce should be used within an hour after it is made. If used after an hour, rewhip slightly.

YIELD: *Generous 2½ cups*

WOODY'S
❦ BREAD PUDDING

Prepared by Karl "Woody" Will, Pastry Chef, Auberge du Soleil, Rutherford, California

"Almost any kind of dry or day-old bread will do. I use it as a means of using up day-old croissants and Danish. The amount of bread added depends on whether you desire a thick, dense pudding or a nice custard with bread on top. I find that about an inch layer of bread in the two-inch pan creates a nice mixture of the two."

Day-old bread, croissants, Danish, or brioche, sliced or cubed, 1-inch layer

1	**cup raisins or other dried fruit, such as cherries**
¼	**cup dark rum**
1	**cup unsalted butter, melted**
2	**cups granulated sugar**
10	**large eggs**
4	**cups heavy or whipping cream**
1	**tablespoon vanilla extract**
1	**tablespoon ground cinnamon**

1. Butter a 9- by 13- by 2-inch baking pan.

2. Soak raisins or other dried fruit in rum for at least 30 minutes.

3. Fill bottom of prepared dish with a 1-inch layer of bread, croissants, or Danish.

4. In a large bowl, whisk melted butter and sugar until incorporated. Whisk in eggs, one at a time, until smooth. Slowly mix in cream until blended.

5. Add vanilla, cinnamon, and dried-fruit mixture and stir until well mixed.

6. Pour custard mixture over bread in prepared pan. Let stand for 30 minutes so that the bread absorbs the liquid.

7. Preheat oven to 325°F.

8. Set pan in a larger ovenproof pan. Add enough hot water to the pan to come halfway up sides of smaller pan.

9. Bake for 30 minutes. Cover pudding pan loosely with aluminum foil to prevent top of pudding from browning too quickly. Bake an additional 25 to 40 minutes, or until custard is set (knife inserted 1 inch from center comes out clean), pudding is puffed, and top is golden brown.

10. Remove from water bath onto a wire rack and cool for 20 minutes.

11. Cut into squares. Serve warm or at room temperature with or without crème anglaise. Serve with Maple Syrup Glaze (recipe follows) if pudding was made from bread or brioche.

Let unused portions come to room temperature, cover, and refrigerate.

YIELD: *15 servings*

Maple Syrup Glaze

Prepared by Karl "Woody" Will

1   **cup pure Vermont maple syrup**
¼   **cup heavy or whipping cream**

1. In a small heavy saucepan over medium-high heat, reduce maple syrup by half, 10 to 15 minutes.

2. Lower heat, add cream, and simmer an additional 5 to 10 minutes.

3. Keep the glaze warm or reheat it in the top of a double boiler over hot, but not boiling, water.

This sauce keeps well in the refrigerator for up to 10 days and can be reheated.

YIELD: *Scant 1 cup*

NOTES

❏ *The pudding will puff up considerably during baking, but will retract as it cools.*
❏ *The recipe was tested with a store-bought raspberry-almond Danish coffee cake, cut into ½-inch-thick slices and placed on the diagonal in the prepared dish. The Danish weighed 1½ pounds.*
❏ *The recipe was tested with a 1-pound bakery brioche, cut into 1-inch cubes.*
❏ *The recipe was also tested with yeast-dough Danish, cut into ½-inch-thick slices. The 4 to 5 individual Danish weighed a total of ¾ pound.*
❏ *In all cases, we used the icing and fruit fillings that were part of the Danish.*
❏ *Cooking time varied depending on quantity of bread. The more bread, the longer the cooking time.*
❏ *The brioche bread pudding was served with Maple Syrup Glaze. The Danish bread puddings were served without a sauce or with Vanilla Custard Sauce (page 53).*

CHOCOLATE
BREAD
PUDDINGS

$\mathbf{B}$read pudding is fine—as long as it's chocolate!"

—*Nancy Baggett*
Author, The International Chocolate Cookbook

CHOCOLATE CHIP
❦ BREAD PUDDING

This pudding looks and tastes like a large, warm, chocolate chip cookie, a delight for kids of all ages.

Day-old French bread, crusts removed, cut into ½-inch cubes to equal 4 cups, 16 to 18 ½-inch-thick slices, about 6 ounces with crusts

2   cups half-and-half
4   tablespoons unsalted butter, cut into small pieces
2   large eggs
½   cup granulated sugar
2   teaspoons vanilla extract
        Pinch of salt
½   teaspoon ground cardamom
½   cup semisweet chocolate chips

NOTES

❏ *If you do not have day-old bread, place fresh bread in a 300°F oven until it begins to lose some of its moisture, or leave fresh bread uncovered to air-dry for several hours or overnight.*
❏ *Milk chocolate chips may be substituted for semisweet.*

1. Lightly butter a 1½-quart soufflé or deep-sided baking dish. Preheat oven to 350°F.

2. In a small heavy saucepan over medium heat, bring half-and-half almost to a boil. Remove from heat. Add butter and stir until completely melted.

3. In a large bowl and with an electric mixer set on medium speed, beat together eggs, sugar, vanilla, salt, and cardamom. Gradually add milk mixture, beating continually until incorporated. Skim and discard foam.

4. Add bread cubes and chocolate chips to custard mixture; with a spoon, toss to combine.

5. Pour pudding mixture into prepared dish.

6. Bake for 45 minutes, or until custard is set (knife inserted 1 inch from center comes out clean), pudding is puffed, and top is browned.

7. Remove from oven onto a wire rack and cool for at least 10 minutes.

8. Spoon onto serving plates. Serve warm with a cold glass of milk.

Let unused portions come to room temperature, cover, and refrigerate.

YIELD: *6 servings*

BOURBON PECAN CHOCOLATE
❦ BREAD PUDDING

Spiked and spirited—a chocoholic's choice—this elegant dessert changes from soufflé to torte as it cools. Vanilla Custard Sauce complements the complex flavors of deep chocolate, bourbon-soaked raisins, crunchy toasted pecans, and hints of cinnamon, nutmeg, and cloves.

Day-old French bread, crusts removed, cut into ½-inch cubes to equal 6 cups, 24 to 27 ½-inch-thick slices, about 9 ounces with crusts

NOTES

❏ *If you do not have day-old bread, place fresh bread in a 300°F oven until it begins to lose some of its moisture, or leave fresh bread uncovered to air-dry for several hours or overnight.*
❏ *Chill for a fudgelike texture.*

⅔	cup raisins
¼	cup Kentucky bourbon
2⅔	cups milk
3	ounces unsweetened chocolate, finely chopped
5	large eggs
1½	cups granulated sugar
1	tablespoon vanilla extract
	Pinch of salt
1	teaspoon ground cinnamon
1	teaspoon grated nutmeg
1	teaspoon ground cloves
⅔	cup chopped pecans, toasted in a 350°F oven for 7 to 10 minutes
6	tablespoons unsalted butter, melted and cooled slightly

1. Generously butter a 2½-quart soufflé dish.

2. Soak raisins in bourbon for at least 30 minutes.

3. In a small heavy saucepan over medium heat, bring milk almost to a boil.

4. In a medium bowl, pour ⅓ cup of the milk over chocolate, stirring until chocolate partially melts and mixture is blended. Add an additional ⅓ cup milk and stir until chocolate melts and mixture is smooth. Add the remaining 2 cups milk, continuing to stir until incorporated.

5. In a large bowl and with an electric mixer set on medium-high speed, beat together eggs, sugar, vanilla, salt, cinnamon, nutmeg, and cloves.

6. Fold chocolate mixture, bread cubes, raisins and bourbon, pecans, and melted butter into egg mixture. Let stand for 1 hour so that the bread absorbs the liquid.

7. Preheat oven to 350°F.

8. Pour pudding mixture into prepared dish. Cover loosely with aluminum foil.

9. Bake for 30 minutes. Uncover and bake for an additional 25 to 30 minutes, or until custard is set (knife inserted 1 inch from center comes out clean) and pudding is puffed.

10. Remove from oven onto a wire rack and cool for at least 30 minutes.

11. Spoon onto serving plates. Serve warm, at room temperature, or chilled with Vanilla Custard Sauce (page 53), 2 to 3 tablespoons sauce for each serving, or sweetened whipped cream.

Let unused portions come to room temperature, cover, and refrigerate.

YIELD: *10 servings*

CHOCOLATE BREAD PUDDING
❦ WITH BRANDY CUSTARD SAUCE

Prepared by Anne Rosenzweig, Executive Chef, Arcadia, New York City

"When I created my chocolate brioche bread pudding, I was looking for a creative, homey, but elegant dish. To achieve a special unctiousness, I used an exquisite Belgian chocolate. As a result, Chocolate Bread Pudding is both familiar and luxurious."

Brioche, 1 12-inch loaf, cut into 12 slices

1   **cup unsalted butter, melted**
8   **ounces bittersweet chocolate, preferably Callebaut, chopped**
3   **cups heavy or whipping cream**
1   **cup milk**
1   **cup granulated sugar**
12 **large egg yolks**
1   **teaspoon vanilla extract**
    Pinch of salt
    Brandy Custard Sauce (recipe follows)

1. Lightly butter a 9- by 13-inch baking dish. Preheat oven to 425°F.

2. Brush bread slices with melted butter and toast in oven until golden brown.

3. Place a large bowl over very hot water. Add chopped chocolate; stir occasionally until chocolate slowly melts.

4. In a medium saucepan, heat cream and milk almost to a boil. Remove from heat.

5. In a large bowl, whisk sugar and yolks until well blended. Slowly whisk in cream mixture. Strain mixture, then skim and discard any foam.

6. Add yolk mixture to melted chocolate, whisking constantly. Stir in vanilla and salt.

7. Place toasted brioche in prepared dish in 2 overlapping rows. Pour chocolate mixture over brioche. Cover with plastic wrap and place smaller pan on top of the pudding so that slices stay submerged. Add weights if necessary. Let stand for 1 hour, or until brioche is soaked through.

8. Preheat oven to 325°F. Remove weights, pan, and plastic wrap from pudding and cover with foil. Punch holes in foil to allow steam to escape. Set the baking dish in a larger pan. Add enough boiling water to the pan to come halfway up sides of baking dish.

9. Bake for 1 hour and 45 minutes, or until liquid has been absorbed and the pudding has a glossy look.

10. Remove from water bath and cool for at least 10 minutes.

11. Cut into squares. Serve warm on a puddle of Brandy Custard Sauce (recipe follows). Serve additional sauce on the side.

Let unused portions come to room temperature, cover, and refrigerate.

YIELD: *12 servings*

Brandy Custard Sauce

Prepared by Anne Rosenzweig

3   large egg yolks
⅓   cup granulated sugar
⅓   cup milk
1   cup heavy or whipping cream
      Pinch of salt
¼   cup brandy

1. In a medium bowl, beat yolks with sugar until well blended.

2. In a medium saucepan, heat milk and cream almost to a boil.

3. Remove from heat and whisk ½ cup cream mixture into yolks and sugar. Slowly whisk yolk mixture back into saucepan of remaining cream and milk.

4. Over medium-low heat, continue to whisk until cream begins to thicken. Do not boil.

5. Remove from heat. Add salt and brandy. Strain into a clean bowl and cool quickly.

6. Serve chilled.

YIELD: *2 cups*

CHOCOLATE ORANGE
❦ BREAD PUDDING

Prepared by Michael Foley, Chef-Proprietor, Printer's Row Restaurant and Le Perroquet, Chicago

"When cooks are looking for the simplest, regional, and even contemporary desserts in American cooking, how could they ever pass up the variations of bread pudding. It's not just the ease of handling, the range from simple vanilla to flavored, it's the lightness, the nutrition, the versatility from meal to snack."

Day-old, firm-textured white bread, 4 slices, crusts removed, cut into ½-inch cubes to equal 2 to 3 cups

NOTE

❑ *Expect the pudding to fall as it cools.*

2	**tablespoons grated orange zest, 2 to 3 oranges**
¼	**teaspoon ground cinnamon**
¼	**teaspoon grated nutmeg**
½	**cup raisins**
1½	**cups milk**
½	**cup granulated sugar**
2	**tablespoons unsweetened cocoa**
8	**tablespoons unsalted butter, cut into small pieces**
4	**large eggs, separated**
½	**cup granulated sugar**
	Confectioners' sugar and unsweetened cocoa, equal amounts combined, enough to dust finished pudding

1. Generously butter the bottom of a 2½-quart soufflé or deep-sided baking dish. Preheat oven to 375°F.

2. In a large bowl, combine bread cubes, zest, cinnamon, nutmeg, and raisins. Set aside.

3. In a small heavy saucepan, combine milk, ½ cup sugar, and cocoa. Bring to a boil over medium heat. Remove from heat and add butter, stirring until butter is melted.

4. In a separate large bowl, whisk yolks. Gradually add milk mixture, whisking continually until incorporated.

5. Pour custard mixture over bread; with a spoon, toss to combine.

6. In a clean, dry, large bowl and with an electric mixer set on medium-low speed, beat egg whites until foamy. Increase mixer speed to medium-high and gradually add ½ cup sugar, beating continuously until stiff but not dry. Gently fold whites into pudding mixture.

7. Pour pudding mixture into prepared dish. Set dish in a larger ovenproof pan. Add enough hot water to the pan to come halfway up sides of baking dish.

8. Bake for 40 to 50 minutes, or until custard is set (knife inserted 1 inch from center comes out clean) and pudding is puffed.

9. Remove from water bath onto a wire rack and cool for at least 10 minutes. Dust with confectioners' sugar and cocoa.

10. Spoon onto serving plates. Serve warm or at room temperature.

Let unused portions come to room temperature, cover, and refrigerate.

YIELD: *8 servings*

CHOCOLATE PEAR
❦ BREAD PUDDING

Create this sophisticated and intensely chocolate pudding for those very special occasions. Brandied pears and deep chocolate custard combine for an elegant finale.

Day-old Italian bread, crusts removed, cut into ½-inch cubes to equal 6 cups, approximately 12 ½-inch-thick slices, about 8 ounces with crusts

1	**cup heavy or whipping cream**
1	**cup milk**
8	**ounces unsweetened chocolate, finely chopped**
4	**large eggs**
½	**cup granulated sugar**
1	**teaspoon vanilla extract**
	Pinch of salt
3	**large, firm Anjou pears**
8	**tablespoons unsalted butter**
2	**tablespoons granulated sugar**
2	**tablespoons brandy**

NOTES

❑ *If you do not have day-old bread, place fresh bread in 300°F oven until it begins to lose some of its moisture, or leave fresh bread uncovered to air-dry for several hours or overnight.*
❑ *To sweeten, use semisweet instead of unsweetened chocolate.*
❑ *Poire Williams may be substituted for brandy.*

1. Lightly butter a 2½-quart soufflé dish.

2. In a small heavy saucepan over medium heat, bring cream and milk almost to a boil.

3. In a medium bowl, pour ½ cup of the cream mixture over chocolate, stirring until chocolate partially melts and mixture is blended. Add an additional ½ cup liquid and stir until chocolate melts and mixture is smooth. Add the remaining cup of liquid, continuing to stir until incorporated.

4. In a large bowl, whisk together eggs, the ½ cup sugar, vanilla, and salt. Gradually add chocolate mixture, whisking continually until incorporated. Set aside.

5. Preheat oven to 350°F.

6. Peel, core, and cut pears into ¼-inch-thick slices.

7. In a large skillet, melt butter and add pears and the 2 tablespoons sugar. Over medium-high heat, sauté pears for 4 minutes. Add brandy and continue to cook for an additional 2 minutes. The pears should remain firm. Remove from heat.

8. Add bread cubes and pears to chocolate mixture; with a spoon, toss to combine.

9. Pour pudding mixture into prepared dish. Set dish in a larger ovenproof pan. Add enough hot water to the pan to come halfway up sides of baking dish.

10. Bake for 1 hour, or until custard is set (knife inserted 1 inch from center comes out clean), pudding is firm to the touch, and top is glossy.

11. Remove from water bath onto a wire rack and cool for at least 10 minutes.

12. Spoon onto serving plates. Serve warm, at room temperature, or chilled with sweetened whipped cream.

Let unused portions come to room temperature, cover, and refrigerate.

YIELD: *10 servings*

FUDGY CHOCOLATE HAZELNUT
❦ BREAD PUDDING

You can't go wrong with a delicious combination of milk chocolate and toasted hazelnuts. Think of this bread pudding as a chocolate bar in a cup. Guests will never guess how simple it is to prepare.

Firm-textured white bread, crusts removed, processed into medium-coarse crumbs to equal 1½ cups, approximately 5 slices

1½	cups milk
¾	cup granulated sugar
6	ounces milk chocolate, finely chopped
1	tablespoon unsalted butter, cut into small pieces
1	large egg
½	cup chopped hazelnuts, toasted in a 350°F oven for 7 to 10 minutes

1. Lightly butter six ½-cup soufflé ramekins. Preheat oven to 350°F.

2. In the top of a double boiler, combine milk, sugar, chocolate, and bread crumbs. Over gently simmering water, cook, stirring occasionally, until chocolate is melted and sugar is dissolved.

3. Remove from heat and add butter. Continue to stir until butter is melted.

4. Whisk egg and gradually add to chocolate mixture; stir until incorporated. Stir in hazelnuts.

5. Pour pudding mixture evenly into prepared ramekins. Set ramekins in an ovenproof pan just large enough to hold them snugly. Add enough hot water to the pan to come halfway up sides of ramekins.

6. Bake for 45 to 50 minutes, or until custard is set (knife inserted off center comes out clean).

7. Remove ramekins from water bath onto a wire rack and cool for at least 10 minutes.

8. Serve in the ramekins, warm or chilled, with sweetened whipped cream.

Let unused portions come to room temperature, cover, and refrigerate.

YIELD: *6 servings*

MEXICAN CHOCOLATE
❦ BREAD PUDDING

Prepared by Kitty Sullivan, Pastry Chef, Cilantros, Del Mar, California

"A super-rich, custardy type of pudding that even people who don't like bread pudding tend to enjoy."

Challah or other egg bread, processed into pea-size or smaller crumbs to equal 3½ cups, approximately 4 slices

2   **cups milk**
3   **ounces unsweetened chocolate, chopped**
6   **ounces good-quality semisweet chocolate, chopped**
4   **large eggs**
¾   **cup granulated sugar**
4   **tablespoons butter, melted**
1   **teaspoon vanilla extract**
¼   **teaspoon salt**
1   **teaspoon freshly ground cinnamon**
1   **cup heavy or whipping cream**
¼   **cup Kahlúa**

1. Generously butter a 2-quart shallow baking dish. Preheat oven to 325°F.

2. In a medium saucepan, bring milk almost to a boil. Remove from heat; add both chocolates and let stand until melted.

3. In a large bowl, combine bread crumbs and chocolate mixture.

4. Add remaining ingredients, one at a time, whisking after each addition until well combined.

5. Pour pudding mixture into prepared dish.

6. Bake for 40 minutes, or until custard is almost set in the center and pudding is puffed.

7. Remove from oven onto a wire rack and cool for 10 minutes.

8. Cut into individual servings. Serve warm with crème anglaise or vanilla gelato.

Let unused portions come to room temperature, cover, and refrigerate.

YIELD: *6 servings*

NOTES

❏ *To serve individually, use six 1-cup soufflé ramekins. Bake for 20 to 25 minutes. Run a knife around inside rim of each ramekin and carefully unmold onto a plate. Invert again onto a serving plate so that the top of the pudding is facing up.*
❏ *The depth of the baking dish will determine the cooking time—the deeper the dish, the longer the pudding needs to cook.*

WHITE CHOCOLATE BREAD PUDDING
❧ WITH WHITE CHOCOLATE SAUCE

Prepared by Dickie Brennan, Chef-Partner of Palace Cafe, New Orleans

"Our parents have developed several famous desserts over the years, like Bananas Foster and Bread Pudding Soufflé, but they say they have never seen a dessert catch on so quickly as our White Chocolate Bread Pudding.

It's only fitting that a variation of a family favorite would become a signature dish."

French bread, 1 loaf, approximately 16 ¼-inch-thick slices, dried in oven

8	**large egg yolks**
2	**large eggs**
½	**cup granulated sugar**
1	**tablespoon vanilla extract**
3	**cups heavy or whipping cream**
1	**cup milk**
10	**ounces white chocolate, finely chopped**
	Chocolate shavings, optional
	White Chocolate Sauce (recipe follows)

1. Lightly butter six 1-cup soufflé ramekins.

2. In a medium bowl, combine yolks, eggs, sugar, vanilla, cream, and milk. Place bowl over a pan of gently simmering water and heat custard mixture until warm. Stir occasionally.

3. Blend in chopped chocolate; continue to stir until chocolate is completely melted.

4. Preheat oven to 275°F.

5. Divide bread equally among prepared ramekins.

6. Pour some of the custard mixture over bread and let settle. When bread absorbs some of the liquid, add remaining custard mixture until ramekins are full.

7. Set ramekins in an ovenproof pan just large enough to hold them snugly. Add enough hot water to the pan to come halfway up sides of ramekins.

8. Cover pan with aluminum foil and bake for 1 hour. Uncover and bake for an additional 15 minutes.

9. Remove from water bath onto a wire rack and cool slightly.

10. Run a knife around inside rim of each ramekin and carefully unmold onto a serving plate. Serve warm or at room temperature with White Chocolate Sauce (recipe follows). Garnish with chocolate shavings.

Let unused portions come to room temperature, cover, and refrigerate.

YIELD: *6 servings*

White Chocolate Sauce

Prepared by Dickie Brennan

⅓ **cup heavy or whipping cream**
8   **ounces white chocolate, finely chopped**

1. In a small heavy saucepan, heat cream until very warm. Remove from heat.

2. Add chocolate and stir until chocolate is completely melted.

3. In the top of a double boiler, keep sauce warm or reheat over hot, but not boiling, water.

This sauce keeps in the refrigerator for up to 10 days and can be reheated.

YIELD: *Scant 1 cup*

WHITE CHOCOLATE MACADAMIA NUT
🦌 BREAD PUDDING

A fancy and rich contemporary dessert, easy to prepare, this is a showstopper. Taste and texture combine for a winning combination of white chocolate and macadamia nuts. The finished pudding is topped with grated white chocolate that melts in your mouth.

Day-old French bread, crusts removed, cut into ¾-inch cubes to equal 4 cups, approximately 10 ¾-inch-thick slices, about 5 to 6 ounces with crusts

4	**large eggs**
½	**cup granulated sugar**
1	**teaspoon vanilla extract**
2	**cups milk**
4	**ounces white chocolate, coarsely chopped, ¾ cup**
½	**cup chopped macadamia nuts**
2	**ounces white chocolate, grated, ⅔ cup**

1. Lightly butter a 1½-quart shallow baking dish.

2. In a large bowl and with an electric mixer set on medium speed, beat together eggs, sugar, and vanilla. Reduce mixer speed to low and add milk; continue beating until well mixed.

3. In a separate large bowl, place bread cubes and the chopped white chocolate. With a fine-mesh sieve, strain custard mixture over bread; with a spoon, toss to combine. Let stand for 15 minutes so that the bread absorbs the liquid.

4. Preheat oven to 375°F.

5. Pour pudding mixture into prepared dish, distributing white chocolate chunks evenly. Sprinkle top with macadamia nuts.

6. Bake for 40 to 45 minutes, or until custard is set (knife inserted 1 inch from center comes out clean), pudding is puffed, and edges are golden brown.

7. Remove from oven onto a wire rack. Immediately sprinkle pudding with the grated white chocolate. Cool for at least 20 minutes.

8. Spoon onto serving plates. Serve warm or at room temperature.

Let unused portions come to room temperature, cover, and refrigerate.

YIELD: *6 servings*

SAVORY BREAD PUDDINGS MADE FROM FRENCH OR ITALIAN BREADS

The idea for savory bread pudding came to me years ago. I was trying to do vegetable soufflés for too many people at a chichi party. The soufflés fell and so we scooped them out and called them 'savory bread pudding' and everyone loved them. Amazing how great dishes are born out of near disaster!"

—*John Ash, Chef-Proprietor,*
John Ash & Co., Santa Rosa, California

OLIVE AND BRIE
❦ APPETIZER BREAD PUDDING

Word will spread about this classy pairing of your favorite assortment of olives and luxurious Brie. This is a first-rate first course or luncheon fare.

Day-old French bread, 4 ½-inch-thick slices, about 1 ounce

4	**ounces Brie cheese, rind removed, at room temperature**
4	**ounces cream cheese, at room temperature**
3	**large eggs**
1	**cup milk**
1	**tablespoon chopped fresh oregano, or 1 teaspoon dried oregano**
1	**cup coarsely chopped pitted olives, of mixed varieties**

1. Generously butter four 1-cup or eight ½-cup soufflé ramekins. Preheat oven to 300°F.

2. Tear bread into small pieces and divide equally among prepared ramekins.

3. In a large bowl and with an electric mixer set on low speed, cream both cheeses until blended.

4. Add eggs, one at a time, beating until thoroughly blended after each addition. Gradually add milk; continue beating until well mixed. Stir in oregano and olives.

5. Pour custard mixture evenly over bread.

6. Set ramekins in an ovenproof pan just large enough to hold them snugly. Add enough hot water to the pan to come halfway up sides of ramekins.

7. Bake for 50 minutes, or until custard is set (knife inserted off center comes out clean) and tops are golden brown.

8. Remove from water bath onto a wire rack and cool for 20 minutes.

9. Serve in the ramekins, warm or at room temperature, with your favorite crisp cracker.

Let unused portions come to room temperature, cover, and refrigerate.

YIELD: *4 light luncheon servings or 8 appetizer servings*

NOTES

❏ *If you do not have day-old bread, place fresh bread in a 300°F oven until it begins to lose some of its moisture, or leave fresh bread uncovered to air-dry for several hours or overnight.*
❏ *The softer the cheeses, the easier it is to combine them. The Brie needs several hours to come to room temperature.*

CURRIED ACORN SQUASH ❦ BREAD PUDDING

Add this out-of-the-ordinary pudding to your autumn buffet. The spunky flavor of curry, the sweetness of brown sugar and apple juice, and the crunchiness from the bits of apple and slices of almonds team perfectly with the winter squash. Seconds anyone?

Day-old French bread, processed into coarse crumbs to equal 2 scant cups, approximately 8 ½-inch-thick slices, about 3 ounces

2	cups puréed cooked acorn squash
4	tablespoons butter, divided
¾	cup finely chopped onion
½	cup finely chopped Granny Smith apple, peeled and cored
¼	cup packed light brown sugar
¼	cup apple juice
2	teaspoons curry powder
3	large eggs
¾	cup half-and-half
¼	teaspoon salt
⅛	teaspoon freshly ground black pepper
2	tablespoons sliced almonds, toasted in a 350°F oven for 5 to 7 minutes

NOTES

❏ *If you do not have day-old bread, place fresh bread in a 300°F oven until it begins to lose some of its moisture, or leave fresh bread uncovered to air-dry for several hours or overnight.*
❏ *Increase or decrease the amount of curry depending on your taste.*
❏ *One large acorn squash, steamed, should yield enough for the 2 cups of purée needed in this recipe.*
❏ *Chicken stock may be substituted for half-and-half. This reduces fat content while changing texture only slightly.*

1. Generously butter a 1-quart soufflé or deep-sided baking dish. Preheat oven to 350°F.

2. Place squash in a large bowl. Set aside.

3. In a medium skillet over medium heat, melt 1 tablespoon of the butter and sauté onion and apple until they begin to soften, 2 minutes. Remove from heat and add to squash.

4. In the same skillet, melt the remaining 3 tablespoons butter. Add brown sugar, apple juice, and curry and cook until sugar dissolves. Set curried syrup aside and cool slightly.

5. In a large bowl and with an electric mixer set on medium speed, beat together eggs, half-and-half, salt, and pepper. Turn off mixer. Add squash, onion, apple, and curried syrup; beat at low speed until well mixed.

6. Add bread crumbs and stir to combine.

7. Pour pudding mixture into prepared dish. Sprinkle top with almonds.

8. Bake for 45 to 50 minutes, or until custard is set (knife inserted 1 inch from center comes out clean), pudding is puffed, and top is golden brown.

9. Remove from oven onto a wire rack and cool for at least 10 minutes.

10. Spoon onto serving plates. Serve warm.

Let unused portions come to room temperature, cover, and refrigerate.

YIELD: *4 light luncheon servings or 8 side dish servings*

GOLDEN CHEESE BREAD SOUFFLÉ
❦ WITH CHUNKY TOMATO BASIL SAUCE

So satisfying, this light yet piquant pudding is suited for brunch, lunch, or dinner. Served with a fresh-tasting tomato sauce, it is destined to become a favorite.

Day-old French bread, 4 ½-inch-thick slices, crusts removed, about 1 ounce with crusts

NOTES

❏ *If you do not have day-old bread, place fresh bread in a 300°F oven until it begins to lose some of its moisture, or leave fresh bread uncovered to air-dry for several hours or overnight.*
❏ *This recipe adapts well to the cholesterol-conscious; simply use the substitutions in parentheses.*
❏ *Expect the bread soufflé to fall as it cools.*

1 **generous tablespoon unsalted butter (unsalted margarine), softened**
8 **ounces soft goat cheese, such as chèvre, at room temperature**
3 **large eggs (¾ cup egg substitute plus 1 large egg white)**
1 **cup milk (skim milk)**
¼ **teaspoon salt**
 Freshly ground black pepper to taste
 Chunky Tomato Basil Sauce (recipe follows)

1. Generously butter (or coat with nonstick vegetable spray) four 1-cup soufflé ramekins. Preheat oven to 300°F.

2. Butter one side of bread slices with the generous 1 tablespoon butter and cut into ½-inch cubes. Divide bread equally among prepared ramekins.

3. In a large bowl and with an electric mixer set on medium-low speed, cream the cheese. Add eggs, one at a time, beating until thoroughly blended after each addition. Reduce mixer speed to low and gradually add milk; continue to beat until well mixed. Beat in salt and pepper.

4. Pour custard mixture evenly over bread.

5. Bake for 1 hour, or until custard is set (knife inserted off center comes out clean), pudding is puffed, and tops are golden brown.

6. Remove from oven onto a wire rack and cool for 5 minutes.

7. Run a knife around inside rim of each ramekin and carefully unmold onto a plate. Invert again onto a serving plate so that the top of the pudding is facing up. Serve warm with Chunky Tomato Basil Sauce (recipe follows), ¼ to ⅓ cup sauce for each serving.

Let unused portions come to room temperature, cover, and refrigerate.

YIELD: *4 servings*

Chunky Tomato Basil Sauce

1   **large garlic clove, quartered**
2   **tablespoons olive oil**
1   **28-ounce can Italian plum tomatoes, drained and chopped**
2   **tablespoons slivered fresh basil, or 2 teaspoons dried basil**
½   **teaspoon salt**
¼   **teaspoon freshly ground black pepper**

1. In a medium skillet over medium heat, sauté garlic in oil until it begins to turn in color, 2 to 4 minutes. Remove garlic and discard.

2. Add tomatoes to oil and bring mixture to a boil. Lower heat and simmer, stirring occasionally, until thickened, 10 minutes.

3. Stir in basil, salt, and pepper.

4. Remove from heat. Cover and keep warm until ready to serve.

This sauce keeps well in the refrigerator for up to 3 days and can be reheated.

YIELD: *Generous 2 cups*

ITALIAN CHICKEN STRATA
❦ WITH PROSCIUTTO AND PINE NUTS

A dressy dish for any occasion, this pudding uses the best of ingredients and blends wonderful flavors. Make when fresh basil and fresh parsley are plentiful.

Italian bread, approximately 7 to 8 ½-inch-thick slices, about 6 ounces

3	tablespoons unsalted butter (unsalted margarine), divided
⅓	cup chopped onion
8	ounces skinless, boneless chicken breasts, cut into 1-inch cubes, 1 cup
4	ounces prosciutto, trimmed of fat and slivered into ¼-inch strips, 1 cup
1	cup seeded and chopped Italian plum tomatoes, 3 medium
6	large eggs (1½ cups egg substitute plus 3 large egg whites)
1¾	cups milk (low-fat milk)
⅓	cup chopped fresh basil, or 1 tablespoon dried basil
2	tablespoons chopped fresh parsley, or 2 teaspoons dried parsley
¼	teaspoon freshly ground black pepper
1	cup grated Parmesan cheese
¼	cup pine nuts, toasted in a 350°F oven for 5 minutes

NOTES

❑ *The depth of the baking dish will determine the cooking time—the deeper the dish, the longer the pudding needs to cook.*
❑ *This recipe adapts well to the cholesterol-conscious; simply use substitutions in parentheses.*
❑ *The taste of the dish is well worth the added expense of prosciutto and pine nuts.*

1. Generously butter (or coat with nonstick vegetable spray) a 2-quart shallow baking dish.

2. Melt 2 tablespoons of the butter and brush one side of bread slices with it. Toast in oven until golden brown. Cut into ½-inch cubes to equal 4 cups. Set aside.

3. In a medium skillet over medium heat, melt the remaining 1 tablespoon butter and sauté onion until soft, 2 minutes. Add chicken and continue cooking until opaque, 5 to 6 minutes, stirring occasionally. Do not overcook. Add the prosciutto and tomatoes and cook an additional 1 to 2 minutes. Remove from heat and set aside.

4. In a large bowl, whisk eggs. Add milk, basil, parsley, and pepper and whisk until well mixed.

5. Place half the bread cubes in prepared pan. Top with half the chicken mixture and half the Parmesan. Repeat layering.

6. Carefully pour custard mixture over bread and cheese. Cover with plastic wrap and press down with your hands or back of a spoon so that the bread absorbs the liquid. Refrigerate several hours or overnight.

7. Preheat oven to 350°F.

8. Remove plastic wrap from pudding. Sprinkle top with pine nuts. Bake for 40 to 55 minutes, or until custard is set (knife inserted 1 inch from center comes out clean), pudding is puffed, and top is golden brown.

9. Remove from oven onto a wire rack and cool for at least 10 minutes.

10. Cut into individual servings. Serve warm with a favorite salad.

Let unused portions come to room temperature, cover, and refrigerate.

YIELD: *6 servings*

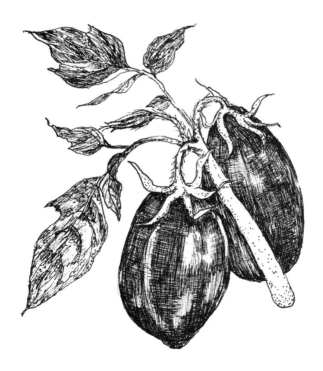

PEPPER AND WILD MUSHROOM PIZZA
❦ BREAD PUDDING

Entertain casually with this shiitake mushroom and red pepper gourmet deep-dish pizza with a French bread crust. Can this be bread pudding?

Day-old French bread, cut into ½-inch cubes to equal 4 generous cups, 15 to 16 ½-inch-thick slices, about 5 to 6 ounces

❑ *If you do not have day-old bread, place fresh bread in a 300°F oven until it begins to lose some of its moisture, or leave fresh bread uncovered to air-dry for several hours or overnight.*
❑ *Fresh shiitake mushrooms may be substituted for dried.*
❑ *Peppers are available in a wide range of colors. Use red and green for Christmas, orange for Halloween, or mix and match.*
❑ *Makes a great snack straight from the refrigerator.*

1   ounce dried shiitake mushrooms
1¼ cups finely chopped scallions, 3 bunches
1½ tablespoons olive oil
2½ cups thinly sliced red pepper strips, 2 peppers
6   large eggs
1¾ cups milk
1½ tablespoons Dijon mustard
1   tablespoon chopped fresh thyme, or 1 teaspoon dried thyme
1   tablespoon chopped fresh oregano, or 1 teaspoon dried oregano
½   teaspoon salt
½   teaspoon freshly ground black pepper
½   teaspoon crushed red pepper flakes
¾   cup grated Parmesan cheese, divided
1½ cups lightly packed, grated mozzarella cheese, 6 ounces

1. Generously butter a 2-quart ceramic quiche or shallow baking dish.

2. Cover mushrooms with hot water and soak for 30 minutes. Drain. Cut off tough stems and discard; slice caps into thin strips.

3. In a large skillet over medium heat, sauté scallions in oil until soft, 1 to 2 minutes. Add pepper strips and cook, stirring occasionally, until tender, 8 minutes. Add mushroom strips and cook an additional 2 minutes. Remove from heat and set aside.

4. Whisk eggs in a large bowl. Add milk, mustard, thyme, oregano, salt, black pepper, and red pepper and whisk until well mixed. Add bread cubes, ½ cup of the Parmesan, and mushroom mixture; with a spoon, toss to combine.

5. Pour pudding mixture into prepared dish. Sprinkle top with mozzarella and the remaining ¼ cup Parmesan. Cover with plastic wrap and press down with your hands or back of a spoon so that the bread absorbs the liquid. Refrigerate several hours or overnight.

6. Preheat oven to 350°F.

7. Remove plastic wrap from pudding. Bake 40 to 45 minutes, or until custard is set (knife inserted 1 inch from center comes out clean), pudding is puffed, and top is golden brown.

8. Remove from oven onto a wire rack and cool for at least 10 minutes.

9. Cut into individual servings. Serve warm or at room temperature.

Let unused portions come to room temperature, cover, and refrigerate.

YIELD: *6 servings*

SCALLOP AND VEGETABLE BREAD PUDDING ❦ WITH RED PEPPER COULIS

Lightly herbed, this successful combination of sautéed vegetables and scallops is a well-bred choice for ladies at lunch. Equally suited as a starter course, accompany each pudding with Red Pepper Coulis.

Day-old French bread, processed into coarse crumbs to equal 2 cups, approximately 9 ½-inch-thick slices, about 3 to 4 ounces

2	tablespoons unsalted butter
1	garlic clove, minced
¼	cup finely chopped onion
¼	cup finely chopped carrots
2	tablespoons finely chopped celery
½	cup finely chopped zucchini
9	ounces sea scallops, about 1 cup, divided
2	large eggs
1	large egg yolk
2½	cups heavy or whipping cream
1	tablespoon fresh tarragon, or 1 teaspoon dried tarragon
1	tablespoon fresh thyme, or 1 teaspoon dried thyme
½	teaspoon salt
¼	teaspoon freshly ground black pepper
	Red Pepper Coulis (recipe follows)

NOTE

❑ *If you do not have day-old bread, place fresh bread in a 300°F oven until it begins to lose some of its moisture, or leave fresh bread uncovered to air-dry for several hours or overnight.*

1. Generously butter six 1-cup soufflé ramekins. Preheat oven to 325°F.

2. In a medium skillet over medium heat, melt butter and sauté garlic, onion, carrots, and celery until they begin to soften, 3 minutes.

3. Add zucchini and cook until crisp-tender, 1 minute. Remove from heat and cool slightly.

4. In a food processor, purée one-third of the scallops. Add eggs, egg yolk, cream, tarragon, thyme, salt, and pepper and pulse custard mixture just until blended.

5. Chop the remaining scallops.

6. In a large bowl, combine the vegetable mixture, custard mixture, chopped scallops, and bread crumbs.

7. Pour pudding mixture evenly into prepared ramekins. Set ramekins in an ovenproof pan just large enough to hold them snugly. Add enough hot water to the pan to come halfway up sides of ramekins.

8. Bake 50 minutes, or until the custard is set (knife inserted off center comes out clean) and tops are golden brown.

9. Remove from oven onto a wire rack and cool for at least 10 minutes.

10. Serve in the ramekins, warm with Red Pepper Coulis (recipe follows), 2 tablespoons sauce for each serving. Pass the extra.

Let unused portions come to room temperature, cover, and refrigerate.

YIELD: *6 servings*

Red Pepper Coulis

3   red bell peppers, seeded and quartered
1   large tomato, seeded and quartered
1   small yellow onion, peeled and quartered
2   garlic cloves
2   tablespoons balsamic vinegar
1   teaspoon granulated sugar
¼   teaspoon salt
½   teaspoon freshly ground black pepper

1. Preheat oven to 450°F.

2. In an ovenproof dish, place peppers, tomato, and onion.

3. Bake for 30 minutes. Add garlic and bake for an additional 15 minutes, or until vegetables are very soft.

4. Remove from oven and cool slightly.

5. Purée vegetables in a food processor. Add vinegar, sugar, salt, and pepper and pulse until blended.

6. Serve warm or at room temperature.

This sauce keeps well in the refrigerator for up to 3 days and can be reheated.

YIELD: *Generous 1½ cups*

TARRAGON
🦃 CHICKEN STRATA

Warm chicken salad with a twist, incorporating bite-size pieces of chicken with shallots, mustard, an abundance of fresh tarragon, and a handful of toasted walnuts.

Day-old French bread, cut into ½-inch cubes to equal 4 cups, 13 to 15 ½-inch-thick slices, about 5 ounces

NOTES

❑ *If you do not have day-old bread, place fresh bread in a 300°F oven until it begins to lose some of its moisture, or leave fresh bread uncovered to air-dry for several hours or overnight.*
❑ *This recipe adapts well to the cholesterol-conscious; simply use the substitutions in parentheses.*

4	**tablespoons mayonnaise (light mayonnaise)**
2	**tablespoons butter (margarine)**
⅓	**cup chopped shallots, 2 medium**
½	**cup chopped celery**
1	**pound skinless, boneless chicken breasts, cut into bite-size pieces, 2 cups**
6	**large eggs (1½ cups egg substitute plus 3 large egg whites)**
1¾	**cups half-and-half (low-fat milk)**
1	**tablespoon Dijon mustard**
⅓	**scant cup chopped fresh tarragon, or 1 tablespoon dried tarragon**
½	**teaspoon salt**
¼	**teaspoon freshly ground black pepper**
¼	**cup chopped walnuts, toasted in a 350°F oven for 7 to 10 minutes**

1. Generously butter (or coat with nonstick vegetable spray) a 2-quart shallow baking dish.

2. In a large bowl, toss bread cubes with mayonnaise. Set aside.

3. In a medium skillet over medium heat, melt butter and sauté shallots and celery until soft, 2 minutes. Add chicken and continue cooking until opaque, 5 to 6 minutes, stirring occasionally. Do not overcook.

4. Whisk eggs in a large bowl. Add half-and-half, mustard, tarragon, salt, and pepper and whisk until well mixed.

5. Place half the bread cubes in prepared pan. Add the chicken mixture. Top with the remaining bread cubes.

6. Pour custard mixture over bread. Cover with plastic wrap and press down with your hands or back of a spoon so that the bread absorbs the liquid. Refrigerate several hours or overnight.

7. Preheat oven to 350°F.

8. Remove plastic wrap from pudding. Sprinkle top with walnuts. Bake for 40 to 45 minutes, or until custard is set (knife inserted

1 inch from center comes out clean), pudding is puffed, and top is golden brown.

9. Remove from oven onto a wire rack and cool for at least 10 minutes.

10. Cut into individual servings. Serve warm with a tarragon vinaigrette.

Let unused portions come to room temperature, cover, and refrigerate.

YIELD: *6 servings*

SAVORY
BREAD PUDDINGS
MADE FROM
BREADS OTHER
THAN FRENCH
OR ITALIAN

T he good news is that everything that's old seems to be new again, and that includes savory bread puddings—thank heaven."

—*Lee Bailey*
Author, Lee Bailey's Tomatoes

PESTO
❦ PUDDING PUFF

It's not a quiche. It's not a casserole. It's a most wonderful puffed bread pudding, an Italian Yorkshire. The basil pesto and sun-dried tomatoes give it the pizzazz of a pizza. Serve as an entrée or alongside plainly dressed meats or fowl.

	Day-old, firm-textured white bread, about 6 slices
¼	**cup basil pesto, homemade or store-bought**
5	**large eggs**
1	**cup milk**
¾	**cup heavy or whipping cream**
1	**garlic clove, minced**
¼	**teaspoon salt**
¼	**cup sun-dried tomatoes, packed in oil and patted dry, coarsely chopped**
1½	**cups lightly packed, grated provolone cheese, 6 ounces**
½	**cup grated Parmesan cheese**

1. Generously butter a 1½-quart soufflé or deep-sided baking dish.

2. Spread pesto on one side of bread slices. Cut bread slices into ½-inch cubes to equal 5 scant cups. Set aside.

3. In a large bowl and with an electric mixer set on medium speed, beat eggs, milk, cream, garlic, and salt until well mixed.

4. Place half the bread cubes in prepared dish. Top with half the tomatoes, half the provolone, and half the Parmesan. Repeat layering.

5. Slowly pour custard mixture over bread and cheese. Cover with plastic wrap and press down with your hands or back of a spoon so that the bread absorbs the liquid. Refrigerate several hours or overnight.

6. Preheat oven to 325°F.

7. Remove plastic wrap and cover pudding with aluminum foil. Bake for 1 hour. Uncover and continue to bake for an additional 10 minutes, or until custard is set (knife inserted 1 inch from center comes out clean), pudding is puffed, and top is golden brown.

8. Remove from oven onto a wire rack and cool for at least 10 minutes.

9. Spoon onto serving plates. Serve warm or at room temperature.

Let unused portions come to room temperature, cover, and refrigerate.

YIELD: *6 servings*

❑ *If you do not have day-old bread, place fresh bread in a 300°F oven until it begins to lose some of its moisture, or leave fresh bread uncovered to air-dry for several hours or overnight.*
❑ *Italian bread may be substituted for the firm-textured white bread. Use 5 scant cups of ½-inch cubes.*
❑ *Expect the pudding puff to fall as it cools.*

BLACK BEAN
🍏 STRATA

Go south of the border for brunch, lunch, or dinner with a popular combination of interesting flavors and cheesy goodness. Make it as hot as you like. Olé!

Sourdough bread, lightly toasted under broiler, cut into ½-inch cubes to equal 4 cups, approximately 5 ½-inch-thick slices, about 7 ounces

½   cup chopped onion
1   tablespoon corn oil
2   cups canned black beans, rinsed and drained
1½   cups seeded and chopped Italian plum tomatoes, 4 to 5
1   4-ounce can chopped mild green chilies, drained
4   tablespoons chopped fresh cilantro
6   large eggs (1½ cups egg substitute plus 3 large egg whites)
1¾   cups half-and-half (low-fat milk)
1   teaspoon ground cumin
½   teaspoon salt
¼   teaspoon cayenne
2½   cups lightly packed, grated Monterey Jack cheese, 10 ounces (1½ cups lightly packed, low-fat grated cheese, 6 ounces)
   Sour cream (low-fat sour cream), as garnish
   Fresh cilantro, chopped, as garnish

1. Lightly oil (or coat with nonstick vegetable spray) a 2-quart shallow baking dish.

2. In a small skillet over medium heat, sauté onion in the 1 tablespoon oil until soft, 2 minutes.

3. In a large bowl, combine bread cubes, onion, beans, tomatoes, chilies, and the 4 tablespoons cilantro.

4. In a separate large bowl, whisk eggs. Add half-and-half, cumin, salt, and cayenne and whisk until well mixed.

5. Place half the bread mixture into prepared dish. Top with half the grated cheese. Repeat layering.

6. Carefully pour custard mixture over bread and cheese. Cover with plastic wrap and press down with your hands or back of a spoon so that the bread absorbs the liquid. Refrigerate several hours or overnight.

7. Preheat oven to 350°F.

❏ *The depth of the baking dish will determine the cooking time—the deeper the dish, the longer the pudding needs to cook.*
❏ *This recipe adapts well to the cholesterol-conscious; simply use the substitutions in parentheses.*
❏ *Two whole canned jalapeño chilies, seeded and chopped, may be substituted for mild green chilies.*
❏ *A 15-ounce can of black beans yields a generous 1½ cups.*

8. Remove plastic wrap from pudding. Bake for 40 to 55 minutes, or until custard is set (knife inserted 1 inch from center comes out clean), pudding is puffed, and top is golden brown.

9. Remove from oven onto a wire rack and cool for at least 10 minutes.

10. Cut into individual servings. Serve warm with sour cream and chopped cilantro.

Let unused portions come to room temperature, cover, and refrigerate.

YIELD: *6 servings*

EGGPLANT, BASIL, AND PARMESAN BREAD PUDDING WITH
❦ CHARRED TOMATO VINAIGRETTE

Prepared by Susan Goss, Chef-Proprietor, Something Different, Indianapolis

"Bread puddings are a great way to use leftovers, both savory and sweet. Once you realize the ratio of bread to custard to 'yummies,' the possibilities are endless!"

Sourdough bread, 10 ounces, cut into 1-inch-thick slices

5	**tablespoons olive oil, divided**
1	**1-pound eggplant, peeled and cut into 1-inch cubes**
3	**tablespoons peeled and minced garlic, 6 large cloves**
3	**cups chopped, well-washed leeks, 2 large**
1½	**cups peeled and chopped tomatoes**
2	**cups shredded Parmesan cheese, divided**
6	**tablespoons chopped fresh basil**
9	**large eggs**
2¼	**cups veal or chicken stock**
	Salt and freshly ground black pepper
	Charred Tomato Vinaigrette (recipe follows)

1. Oil a 9- by 9- by 2-inch baking pan or 3-quart soufflé dish. Preheat grill or broiler.

2. Brush both sides of bread slices with 2 tablespoons of the olive oil. Toast bread on grill or under broiler until crisp on both sides. Cut into 1-inch cubes. Set aside.

3. Toss eggplant cubes with 2 tablespoons of the olive oil. Grill or roast in a 375°F preheated oven until tender. Set aside.

4. In a large skillet, sauté garlic and leek in the remaining 1 tablespoon olive oil until soft and golden.

5. In a large bowl, combine eggplant, bread cubes, leek mixture, tomatoes, 1 cup of the cheese, and basil and mix well.

6. In a separate large bowl, whisk eggs with stock and add salt and pepper to taste.

7. Combine eggplant and egg mixtures, tossing well.

8. Pour pudding mixture into prepared pan. Sprinkle top with the remaining 1 cup cheese.

9. Bake for 30 to 45 minutes, or until custard is set (knife inserted 1 inch from center comes out clean) and pudding is puffed.

10. Remove from oven and cool for at least 10 minutes.

11. Serve warm, at room temperature, or cold with Charred Tomato Vinaigrette (recipe follows).

Let unused portions come to room temperature, cover, and refrigerate.

YIELD: *8 servings*

Charred Tomato Vinaigrette

Prepared by Susan Goss

1   **pound Italian plum tomatoes, 7 medium**
½   **cup balsamic vinegar**
1½   **cups olive oil**
½   **teaspoon kosher salt**
¼   **teaspoon freshly ground black pepper**

1. Preheat grill or broiler. Grill or broil tomatoes until charred on all sides.

2. In a food processor, purée tomatoes with skins. With machine running, add vinegar and oil.

3. Season with salt and pepper.

4. Refrigerate until ready to use.

The vinaigrette will keep one week chilled.

YIELD: *3 cups*

SAVORY PEAR AND HAVARTI
❦ BRUNCH BREAD PUDDING

Don't shy away from this compatible combination of pepper-spiked fruit and creamy cheese, complemented with warm maple syrup. Although its name suggests brunch, how about serving this dish for Sunday supper with smoked meats?

Day-old, firm-textured white bread, 1-pound loaf, approximately 16 slices

3	tablespoons butter (margarine)
3	pounds Bartlett pears, peeled, cored, and cut into ⅜-inch-thick slices
3	tablespoons granulated sugar
¼	teaspoon coarsely ground black pepper
2	tablespoons fresh lemon juice
1½	cups milk (skim milk)
1½	cups heavy or whipping cream (half-and-half)
4	large eggs (1 cup egg substitute plus 2 large egg whites)
1	tablespoon honey mustard
6	tablespoons butter (margarine), melted
2	cups lightly packed, grated Havarti cheese, 8 ounces
1¼	teaspoons coarsely ground black pepper

NOTES

❑ *If you do not have day-old bread, place fresh bread in a 300°F oven until it begins to lose some of its moisture, or leave fresh bread uncovered to air-dry for several hours or overnight.*
❑ *This recipe adapts well to the cholesterol-conscious; simply use substitutions in parentheses.*
❑ *Cover loosely with aluminum foil if pudding browns too quickly.*

1. Generously butter (or coat with nonstick vegetable spray) a 2½-quart shallow baking dish.

2. In a large skillet over medium heat, melt the 3 tablespoons butter and sauté pears until they begin to turn in color, 3 minutes. Increase heat to medium-high and sprinkle pears with sugar, stirring for 3 minutes.

3. Add the ¼ teaspoon pepper and lemon juice. Boil for 3 minutes, stirring constantly. Remove from heat and cool to lukewarm.

4. In a small heavy saucepan over medium heat, bring milk and cream almost to a boil.

5. In a large bowl, whisk together eggs and mustard. Gradually add milk mixture, whisking continually until incorporated.

6. Brush one side of bread slices with the 6 tablespoons melted butter. Cut enough pear shapes from bread slices to decorate top of pudding. Cut the leftover bread into ½-inch cubes.

7. Place half the bread cubes in the prepared dish. Top with half the cheese, half the pears, and ¾ teaspoon pepper. Repeat layering. Top with the bread pear shapes, buttered side up, and the remaining ½ teaspoon pepper.

8. Carefully pour custard mixture over bread, cheese, and pears. Let stand for 30 minutes so that the bread absorbs the liquid.

9. Preheat oven to 350°F.

10. Set dish in a larger ovenproof pan. Add enough hot water to the pan to come halfway up sides of baking dish.

11. Bake for 1 hour, or until custard is set (knife inserted 1 inch from center comes out clean), pudding is puffed, and top is golden brown.

12. Remove from oven onto a wire rack and cool for 20 minutes.

13. Cut into individual servings and serve with warm maple syrup.

Let unused portions come to room temperature, cover, and refrigerate.

YIELD: *8 servings*

TURKEY SEMISTRATA
❦ WITH CASEY'S CANDIED CRANBERRIES

Don't prepare this only on the day after Thanksgiving. Treat yourself on any weekend to our version of a baked club sandwich: turkey with melted fontina cheese and smoky bacon. The candied cranberries are a must with their perky personality.

Firm-textured white bread, toasted until golden brown, cut into ½-inch cubes to equal 4 cups, about 7 slices

NOTE

❏ *The depth of the baking dish will determine the cooking time—the deeper the dish, the longer the pudding needs to cook.*

4	**tablespoons Durkee's Famous Sauce**
1	**tablespoon unsalted butter**
½	**cup thinly sliced scallions**
5	**large eggs**
1½	**cups milk**
2	**teaspoons herbes de Provence**
	Pinch of salt
¼	**teaspoon freshly ground black pepper**
8	**ounces cooked turkey, shredded, 2 cups**
1½	**cups lightly packed, grated fontina cheese, 6 ounces, divided**
6	**slices bacon, cooked and crumbled**
	Casey's Candied Cranberries (recipe follows)

1. Generously butter a 2-quart shallow baking dish.

2. Toss bread cubes with Durkee's and set aside.

3. In a medium skillet over medium heat, melt butter and sauté scallions until soft, 1 minute. Remove from heat and set aside.

4. Whisk eggs in a large bowl. Add milk, herbes de Provence, salt, and pepper and whisk until well mixed. Add bread cubes, scallions, turkey, and half the cheese to custard mixture; with a spoon, toss to combine.

5. Pour pudding mixture into prepared dish. Top with the remaining cheese. Cover with plastic wrap and press down with your hands or back of a spoon so that the bread absorbs the liquid. Refrigerate several hours or overnight.

6. Preheat oven to 350°F.

7. Remove plastic wrap from pudding. Top with bacon. Bake for 40 to 55 minutes, or until custard is set (knife inserted 1 inch from center comes out clean), pudding is puffed, and top is golden brown.

8. Remove from oven onto a wire rack and cool for at least 10 minutes.

9. Cut into individual servings. Serve warm with Casey's Candied Cranberries (recipe follows), ½ cup cranberries for each serving.

Let unused portions come to room temperature, cover, and refrigerate.

YIELD: *6 servings*

Casey's Candied Cranberries

1   cup water
1   cup granulated sugar
    Slivered rind of 1 orange
4   cups fresh cranberries
3   whole cloves
1   cinnamon stick

1. In a medium-size heavy saucepan, combine water and sugar. Over medium-high heat, bring to a boil, stirring until sugar is dissolved.

2. Add orange rind and continue cooking until syrup begins to thicken, 10 minutes. Remove rind and set aside on waxed paper.

3. Reduce heat and add cranberries, cloves, and cinnamon stick. Over low heat, cook until cranberries begin to pop, 5 to 7 minutes. With a slotted spoon, remove cranberries to a serving bowl.

4. Increase heat to medium and cook until syrup is thick, 10 to 12 minutes. Remove from heat, discard cloves and cinnamon stick, and pour syrup over cranberries.

5. Cool to room temperature. Cover and refrigerate several hours or overnight. When ready to use, serve chilled, topped with orange rind.

YIELD: *3 cups*

WELSH RAREBIT
❦ SINGLE STRATA

Prepared by Steven Keneipp, Chef-Proprietor, The Classic Kitchen, Noblesville, Indiana

"Keeping alive an old tradition, this recipe was adapted from an old reprint of an eighteenth-century cookbook. You could have dined on this two centuries ago and it would have tasted the same."

Whole wheat bread, 8 slices

3	tablespoons unsalted butter
3	tablespoons all-purpose flour
1	tablespoon Coleman's dry mustard
¾	teaspoon freshly ground black pepper
6	tablespoons half-and-half
¾	cup English dark ale or dark beer
1½	teaspoons Worcestershire sauce
1¼	pounds mild Cheddar cheese, grated, 5 cups
	Fresh mushrooms, sliced
	Cherry tomatoes, quartered

1. In a heavy 3-quart saucepan, heat butter until melted. Stir in flour, mustard, and black pepper and cook a few minutes.

2. Whisk in half-and-half, ale, and Worcestershire sauce and cook an additional few minutes until somewhat thickened.

3. Stir in cheese and continue stirring until it melts and mixture is smooth. Refrigerate until needed.

4. Preheat oven to 425°F. Lightly butter eight individual gratin dishes.

5. Toast whole wheat bread slices and cut into points (on the diagonal into quarters).

6. Place 1 toast slice (4 points) in each prepared dish and top with mushrooms and tomatoes. Top with cheese mixture.

7. Bake for 10 to 15 minutes, or until cheese melts and begins to bubble.

8. Remove from oven and cool slightly.

9. Serve warm in the gratin dishes—delicious with minted peas.

The individual rarebits may be covered and refrigerated after preparation. When needed, uncover and bake.

YIELD: *8 servings*

SAVORY
BREAD PUDDINGS
MADE FROM
NOVELTY
BREADS

The best thing I've heard lately about eating healthy is, two pieces of bread with every meal, whether it's straight or struted in your strata."

—*Julee Rosso, coauthor,*
The Silver Palate Cookbooks *and*
The New Basics Cookbook, *and author,*
Great Good Food—Luscious Lower-Fat Cooking

CONFETTI
❦ CORN PUDDING

Corn pudding plus red onion, red pepper, scallions, and fresh thyme result in a refined side dish that can stand alone. When looking for a match for grilled meats or fish, stop here.

Corn bread stuffing (packaged dry mix), 1 cup

1	**tablespoon unsalted butter**
⅓	**cup finely chopped red onion**
⅓	**cup finely chopped scallions**
⅓	**cup finely chopped red pepper**
3	**large eggs (1¼ cups egg substitute plus 2 large egg whites)**
2	**large egg yolks (omit)**
1¾	**cups heavy or whipping cream (skim milk)**
2	**teaspoons fresh thyme**
½	**teaspoon salt**
⅛	**teaspoon ground white pepper**
1	**10-ounce package frozen corn, thawed**

NOTES

❑ *This recipe adapts well to the cholesterol-conscious; simply use substitutions in parentheses.*
❑ *One tablespoon chopped fresh chives may be substituted for the scallions. Add with the thyme.*

1. Generously butter (or coat with a nonstick vegetable spray) a 1½-quart soufflé or deep-sided baking dish. Preheat oven to 350°F.

2. In a small skillet over medium heat, melt butter and sauté red onion, scallions, and red pepper until they begin to soften, 2 minutes. Remove from heat and set aside.

3. In a large bowl and with an electric mixer set on medium speed, beat eggs, egg yolks, cream, thyme, salt, and pepper until well mixed.

4. Add corn, corn bread stuffing, and onion mixture to custard mixture. Stir to combine.

5. Pour pudding mixture into prepared dish. Set dish in a larger ovenproof pan. Add enough hot water to the pan to come halfway up sides of baking dish.

6. Bake for 1 hour and 5 to 10 minutes, or until custard is set (knife inserted 1 inch from center comes out clean), pudding is puffed, and top is golden brown.

7. Remove from water bath onto a wire rack and cool for at least 10 minutes.

8. Spoon onto serving plates. Serve warm or at room temperature.

Let unused portions come to room temperature, cover, and refrigerate.

YIELD: *4 light luncheon servings or 8 side dish servings*

JACK'S THANKSGIVING
❦ BREAD PUDDING

Barbara's husband, Jack, traditionally makes the best Thanksgiving dressing. Yes, it's bread pudding and too good to have just once a year. Serve with or without your favorite bird.

Herb stuffing (packaged dry mix), 4 cups, 8 ounces

8	ounces mild pork sausage
2	tablespoons butter
1	garlic clove, crushed
1	cup finely chopped celery, stalks and leaves
½	cup chopped onion
½	cup chopped fresh mushrooms
1	cup chopped fresh parsley
1	cup chopped green pepper
1	cup slivered almonds
4	large eggs
¾	cup canned, condensed consommé
¾	cup Madeira
½	teaspoon poultry seasoning
¼	teaspoon grated nutmeg
½	teaspoon salt
¼	teaspoon freshly ground black pepper
	Pinch of cayenne

1. Lightly butter a 2-quart shallow baking dish.

2. In a large skillet over medium heat, sauté sausage until completely browned. With a slotted spoon, remove sausage to a large bowl. Set aside.

3. Preheat oven to 350°F.

4. In the same skillet, melt butter and add garlic, celery, onion, mushrooms, parsley, green pepper, almonds, and stuffing. Cook gently, stirring occasionally, until onion begins to soften, 10 minutes. Remove from heat and add to sausage.

5. Whisk eggs in a separate large bowl. Add consommé, Madeira, poultry seasoning, nutmeg, salt, pepper, and cayenne and whisk until well mixed. Add to stuffing mixture; with a spoon, toss to combine.

6. Pour pudding mixture into the prepared dish. Cover with alu-

aluminum foil and bake for 45 to 55 minutes.

7. Remove from oven and serve immediately or keep warm until ready to serve.

Let unused portions come to room temperature, cover, and refrigerate.

YIELD: *8 side dish servings*

ROSE'S BAGEL AND LOX CREAM CHEESE ❦ CUSTARD BREAD PUDDING

Serve a generous slice of this unique version of a brunch favorite to weekend guests. Accompany with a crisp green salad and plenty of fresh fruit. Compliments are guaranteed to follow.

Bagel, 1 large, cut in half to produce two half-moon-shape pieces, each half cut into four horizontal slices, 8 thin slices in total

1	**generous tablespoon butter, softened**
4	**ounces cream cheese, at room temperature**
3	**large eggs**
1	**cup milk**
½	**cup heavy or whipping cream**
¼	**teaspoon dried dill**
2	**ounces lox or smoked salmon, cut with scissors into small pieces**

1. Lightly butter a 1½-quart glass loaf pan.

2. Spread one side of half-moon-shape bagel slices with the 1 tablespoon butter. Arrange bagel slices, buttered side up, in prepared pan in an overlapping pattern, fallen-domino fashion.

3. In a large bowl and with an electric mixer set on medium-low speed, cream the cheese. Add eggs, one at a time, beating until thoroughly blended after each addition. Reduce mixer speed to low and gradually add milk and cream; continue beating until well mixed. Beat in dill and salmon.

4. Carefully pour custard mixture over bagel slices. Cover with plastic wrap and place smaller pan on top of pudding mixture so that bagel slices stay submerged. Refrigerate several hours or overnight.

5. Preheat oven to 300°F.

6. Remove pan and plastic wrap from pudding. Set loaf pan in a larger ovenproof pan. Add enough hot water to the pan to come halfway up sides of loaf pan.

7. Bake for 1 hour, or until custard is set (knife inserted 1 inch from center comes out clean).

8. Remove from water bath onto a wire rack and cool for 30 minutes.

9. Cut into slices. Serve warm, at room temperature, or chilled.

Let unused portions come to room temperature, cover, and refrigerate.

YIELD: *6 servings*

INDEX